SEARCHERS, SEERS, & SHAKERS

SEARCHERS, SEERS, & SHAKERS

MASTERS OF SOCIAL SCIENCE

JAMES A. SCHELLENBERG

Transaction Publishers
New Brunswick (U.S.A.) and London (U.K.)

Library of Congress Catalog Number: 2006051099
ISBN: 0-7658-0350-X
       978-0-7658-0350-4
Printed in the United States of America

Library of Congress Cataloging-in-Publication Data

Schellenberg, James., A. 1932-
    Searchers, seers, and shakers : masters of social science / James A. Schellenberg.
        p. cm.
    Includes bibliographical references and index.
    Contents: Discovers—Theorists—Reformers.
    ISBN 0-7658-0350-X (alk. paper)
        1. Social scientists—Biography.   2. Social sciences—History—20th century.   I. Title.

H57.S34   2006
300.92'2—dc22   2006051099
[B]

Contents

Preface

This work has been developing for more than half a century. It was during my college days, way back in the early 1950s, that I came across *The Proper Study of Mankind*. This book by Stuart Chase, published in 1948, gave a popular overview of developments in the social sciences. It made me want to become a social scientist.

Several of my undergraduate teachers were also prime influences. Two of these were sociology professors, and sociology became my major field. I saw this not only as an interesting field of study, but as a core area for the social sciences. Sociology continued to be my major when I did graduate work at the University of Kansas, but my interests ranged over a much broader area. I saw myself first as a social scientist—intent on applying the methods of science to the understanding of human societies—and only secondarily as a sociologist. I took a great deal of psychology to support my sociology major, for I felt that social psychology was central among the behavioral sciences. By becoming a sociologist and social psychologist I felt ready to tackle the central questions of the social sciences—such as the distinctively human way of becoming social, how behavior is framed by the cultural context, how groups set themselves apart in different ways, and how they may come into conflict with each other. Of course, I focused on specific questions for study (such as mate selection for my doctoral dissertation, and the effects of group size in another early work). However, at the back of my mind was always the conviction that the social sciences had a basic unity, and I intended that my own career would be directed to understanding this unity.

In 1974, I went to Ireland for a year as a visiting professor. The plan was to spend the fall in the North, and the following spring in the Republic. During this time I would be giving my research attention to the conflict in Northern Ireland. But what was I to offer in return? In preparing lectures that I could use in Ireland, I formed what might be called a "biographical approach" to social psychology. I could give general lectures on the lives and ideas of several of the intellectual giants of the field. These could be used both in my psychology placement in the North (at Coleraine's New University of Ulster) and in my sociology teaching in the South (at University College, Cork).

After returning from my year in Ireland, I adapted my lecture materials into a book, *Masters of Social Psychology,* published in 1978. Here I presented several main approaches to social psychology by looking at the lives and thoughts of four "masters"-- Sigmund Freud, George H. Mead, Kurt Lewin, and B. F. Skinner. This book received a generally favorable response, and was ultimately translated into several languages other than English. From this effort I concluded that the biographical approach was at least one useful way to explore ideas in the social sciences.

As my career continued at Western Michigan University and Indiana State University, I pursued a broad range of research and teaching. Ultimately the study of social conflict and conflict resolution became my central focus. In two of my books in this area (in *The Science of Conflict,* published in 1982, and in *Conflict Resolution,* which appeared in 1996) I used a biographical approach in some of the chapters. I felt that looking at the lives of key people helped to describe their ideas and influences. This in turn helped me to clarify several main approaches to the study of social conflict.

As I embarked on plans for the present book, two central convictions were in the back of my mind. One was that there is a fundamental unity behind the various forms of social science. There is a general *social science* as well as a variety of social science *disciplines.* My second conviction was that a biographical approach was a useful tool for making clear some of the central ideas of social science. By looking at the lives and ideas of selected "masters," we should be better able to understand the fundamental nature (or natures) of social science.

Then came the most interesting part. I read about the lives of many of the leading social scientists of the twentieth century. Finally, I selected eleven for special attention. These are the persons treated at length in this book—Louis and Mary Leakey, Margaret Mead, B.F. Skinner, John Dewey, Talcott Parsons, Kenneth Boulding, Gunnar and Alva Myrdal, C. Wright Mills, and Daniel P. Moynihan. I also looked at two men from earlier centuries (the Marquis de Condorcet and Auguste Comte) who helped set the stage for modern social science.

Certainly there are other men and women who have had a tremendous impact on social science. But I feel that my selections at least serve to illustrate the broad nature of social science—including the discovery of new understandings, the development of theories about them, and applications of our knowledge toward the betterment of human society.

J.A.S.

Part 1

Introduction

1

The Coming of Social Science

Mathematician and Philosopher

Born in northern France in 1743, he was christened with a long name: Marie Jean Antoine Nicolas de Caritat. Soon, however, he became known as the Marquis de Condorcet, for he was born into the French nobility. His father, a French cavalry officer, died before Condorcet was five years old. His mother, a deeply religious woman, consecrated her frail child to the Virgin Mary and saw that he had the very best education provided by Jesuit schools. To further protect him, she tried to isolate him from other boys and saw that he wore only girls' clothes till he was nine years old. Extremely shy as a boy, he became as a man what one biographer has described as "extremely refined with a craving for intimacy and affection to which was joined indecision, a certain timidity, and a dangerous impressionability."[1]

In 1758, Condorcet was sent to Paris to further his education. His associations at the Jesuit school there were limited mostly to teachers and books. He showed a special interest in mathematics, and presented learned papers in this subject while still a teenager. When he completed his formal education, he decided, much to the dismay of his family, to pursue a career as a professional mathematician. In 1765, he published his first work, *Essay on Integral Calculus*. Soon he was known as one of the leading French mathematicians and as such was welcomed into the intellectual circles of Paris. He was supported very modestly there through an allowance from his mother.

This was the Age of Enlightenment. Established forms were being questioned everywhere, and in no country was the contrast greater than in France between the new forces and those established by the past. The interests of the rising groups of businessmen, industrialists, and professionals challenged the Old Regime of the monarchy, the Catholic Church, and the privileges of the nobility. In Paris, the intellectual center

3

of the world at that time, it became fashionable to be critical of everything, even in the salons of the nobility. Those persons of letters who led the questioning and promoted a new Age of Reason became known as *philosophes*. They included leading scholars such as Voltaire, Montesquieu, Rousseau, Diderot, and Turgot. They also included hundreds of lesser-known intellectuals, and Condorcet soon became one of these.

Condorcet was awkward in the atmosphere of the fashionable gatherings in private salons. He was more at home in the company of individual scholars, who recognized his outstanding ability in mathematics. But he was not content to be just a mathematician; he aspired to become a full-fledged philosopher. Grounded in the rational disciplines of mathematics, he sought to apply the dictates of reason to everything in the world.

Condorcet later was to summarize the central ideas of the *philosophes* as "always proclaiming the independence of reason and the freedom of thought as the salvation of mankind." Behind these ideas were the assumptions that nature (including human nature) is fundamentally benign, and that it can be accurately perceived through science and reason when the freedom of thought is allowed to flourish. Furthermore, it was assumed that despite the impediments of traditional forms, humans had certain natural rights upon which a proper social order must be based. Later these became enumerated as the rights of life, liberty, and the pursuit of happiness in the American Revolution's *Declaration of Independence* or, in the French Revolution's *Declaration of the Rights of Man and of the Citizen*, as liberty, property, security, and resistance to oppression.[2]

A special boost for the fortunes of the *philosophes* came in 1774 when one of them, Jacques Turgot, was appointed minister of finance by King Louis XVI. Here was the opportunity to put into practice reform measures inspired by the ideals of free trade. When chosen by Turgot for the post of inspector of the mint (or, in effect, controller general of France), Condorcet was given the opportunity to move into a governmental residence, receive a respectable salary, and take on the mission of economic reform. He wrote papers advocating the abolition of all restrictions on trade and labor and generally helped his friend (Turgot was the fellow *philosophe* that he most idealized) carry out new economic policies. Pressures from the nobility, however, soon were arrayed against Turgot, and he was replaced after only two years by a man who was more tolerant of internal tariffs. Condorcet immediately resigned his position, writing to Voltaire "We have had a beautiful dream, but it has been brief. I am going back to geometry and philosophy."[3]

Later Condorcet was to resume his duties as inspector of the mint, but with fewer opportunities to influence economic policies. Meanwhile, he continued to be recognized as a mathematician and philosopher. Having been elected in 1769 to membership in the French Academy of Science, he served that body as secretary for most of the remaining years of his life.

In 1786 Condorcet met, fell in love with, and married a woman named Sophie, the daughter of the Marquis de Grouchy. She has been described as, at the time, "beautiful, refined, intelligent, enlightened, rich, and twenty-two." In any event, the two of them appeared to have had a very happy marriage, blessed by one child, a daughter born in 1790. The Condorcet household, inspired by the grace of the young wife and with the increasingly free spirit of the husband, became a center for gatherings of the intelligentsia of Paris. Distinguished guests from other countries were also made welcome, including Adam Smith of Great Britain and Thomas Jefferson from America.[4]

The Revolutionary

Condorcet had been an advocate of social revolution long before the beginning of the French Revolution, and he also favored rather drastic measures for political reform. But he was a pacifist by nature, and his public statements never supported violent methods of change. The political system he favored—before the Revolution—could be best characterized as a constitutional monarchy. It should include, he felt, such forms as the direct election of national legislators from those who held property, decentralized forms of local government, a minimum of governmental restrictions in economic affairs, women's suffrage, full citizenship rights for members of all races, universal public education, and an absolute freedom of thought. He was strongly opposed to any recognized political role for the Church. All of these were clear elements of Condorcet's political philosophy before the Revolution.

In most basic respects Condorcet's political philosophy remained unchanged until the time of his death. He was always the rationalist, calmly trying to identify through intellectual analysis the best forms of political organization and action. But he also changed in important ways, coming to advocate the removal of the monarchy and the establishment of a national democracy.

Condorcet was the only one of the *philosophes* to take an active part in the French Revolution, since by then all other major figures of that movement had died. Condorcet was not at first in favor of the move when, facing economic woes, the king called for a meeting of the Estates General in 1789, since that body recognized the formal power of the nobility and clergy. He would have preferred a more direct role for popular participation. But when the Third Estate seceded from the Estates General to form the National Assembly, Condorcet fully approved. He took the opportunity to draft a rather elaborate Declaration of Rights which he proposed to the Assembly, and this later became summarized by a more simply stated *Declaration of the Rights of Man and the Citizen.*

Impressed by the popular uprising which led to the Fall of the Bastille on July 14, 1789, Condorcet soon became convinced that the monarchy should be replaced by a republican form of government. He renounced his noble title and became elected, in 1791, to the municipal council of Paris. In this role he sought to influence the national reforms of the newly established Constituent Assembly. His plan for governmental finance was approved by the Assembly in 1791. During the short period of the Legislative Assembly (October 1791, to September 20, 1792) he became a more active leader, serving eventually as president of that body. Condorcet then kept busy drafting proclamations and making addresses, but he was not very persuasive. His manner of speaking has been described as "cold and awkward," with gestures "restrained and weary" and lacking "spontaneity and variety." Nevertheless, he was highly respected because of his reputation and character.[5]

When elections to the new National Convention were held late in 1792, Condorcet was easily elected to a seat. But the uprising of the Paris mob had grown, and he was confused by the sudden declaration of the Republic on September 21. He opposed the subsequent attempts to try (and eventually behead) the king. The Convention soon became the setting for a fierce battle between two factions, the Girondins and the more radical Jacobins. Condorcet avoided any formal tie to either group, though it soon became clear that the Jacobins considered him part of the enemy. Nevertheless, he attempted to draft a constitution for the Republic. It was a lengthy document which won the support of most Girondins, but the Jacobins were harshly critical. Their leader Robespierre had only contempt for the document. He told Condorcet that it appeared "designed not for mankind, but for the rich, for monopolists, for stock jobbers, and for tyrants."[6]

Jacobin leaders drafted a new constitution, which was formally approved on June 24, 1793. The Girondins, now expelled by the Convention, were subject to trial as traitors to the Republic. Condorcet wrote energetically against the new constitution, and for these efforts, on July

8, he was added to the list of those subject to arrest. In hopes of aiding him to escape the guillotine, his friends arranged that he find refuge in a small pension kept by a Madame Vernet. As the weeks there turned into months, he determined to make use of his time by writing.

Condorcet's Vision

During the nine months he was in hiding at the home of Madame Vernet, Condorcet frequently heard news about formerly close associates who met their death at the guillotine. That too, it appeared, would be his fate, if and when he might be found. But he sought to put his time to more creative use than worries about his personal safety. Using whatever materials he could find for writing, he began to record his own experiences, seeking to justify the role he had played. But he soon abandoned this attempt in favor of something much more ambitious. He would put the Revolution itself into its broad historical context. Never mind the tragic events then being experienced by his country and by himself personally; he could spend his time contemplating the broader issues about human existence. By retelling his version of the history of the world, he could show how the future was bound to be brighter. He could show how the ideals of the Revolution—that faith directed to Nature, Reason, and Humanity rather than the old religious ideas—would prove triumphant in the end.

Condorcet's *Sketch of an Historical Picture of the Progress of the Human Mind* divides human history into nine main periods or epochs. These show how mankind has gradually increased in the knowledge of the world and has made this knowledge ever more useful for human society. For example, his eighth epoch began with the invention of printing and continued until the philosophical contributions of René Descartes. Printing became a way that knowledge could be preserved and given almost unlimited circulation. This diffusion of knowledge made it impossible for significant contributions to be lost and helped to develop a better educated populace. Further, it provided for more rational discourse and inspired new scientific contributions, such as those of Copernicus and Galileo.[7]

After Descartes, ever more rational discourse could be encouraged. This led to the discovery of basic laws of the universe by Isaac Newton. Also, the fundamental laws of the mind, based on the human senses and their combinations, were put forward by John Locke. Such psychological knowledge could lead to truth in the social sciences as certain as were the truths of natural science. This great ninth epoch brought us to the

French Revolution, which, with its great ideals of reason and freedom, would usher in a new pattern of society.

The next epoch would be one of almost unlimited progress, with human equality (between nations, between classes, and between individuals) as a key theme. True, there would continue to be setbacks now and then. Progress, though it "at present may appear chimerical," will inevitably be the story of the future. Truth, he said, "in spite of the transient success of prejudices, and the support they receive from the corruption of governments or of the people, must in the end obtain a durable triumph" for "nature has indissolubly united the advancement of knowledge with the progress of liberty, virtue, and respect for the natural rights of man."[8]

The main theme of his essay, as stated in its introduction, is that "no bounds have been fixed on the improvement of the human faculties; that the perfectibility of man is absolutely indefinite; that the progress of this perfectibility, henceforth above the control of every power that would impede it, has no other limit than the duration of the globe upon which nature has placed us."[9]

Such is the vision of scientific optimism produced by Condorcet as he hid from his enemies during the most violent period of the French Revolution. His optimism was based primarily on the growth of knowledge made possible by modern science. But it was also based on the methods and ideas of science extending more and more into the realm of human society. He thus envisaged the development of a social science tied together firmly with the advances of natural science. For man is a part of nature, and the methods of science must be extended to humans and their society as well as to the study of physical matter in motion. His prophecies concerning the betterment of humanity reserved a clear place for the development of social science.

As news came of many of his former associates being executed, Condorcet became increasingly concerned about his safety. He was also especially concerned about the safety of his benefactress, for Madame Vernet would surely be punished if found to be harboring a fugitive. Perhaps it is characteristic of Condorcet that he seemed more concerned about another person than for his own life as he began plans for an escape.

Madame Vernet strongly opposed his leaving. She said to him: "The Convention has the power to put you outside the law, but it has not the power to put you outside of humanity. You will remain."[10]

Finally, eluding his protector, Condorcet left the house in disguise. For several days he avoided capture, then was discovered after hungrily seeking food at an inn. His stay in prison was brief, for the very next morning, on April 8, 1794, he was found dead in his cell. Apparently (though some scholars have speculated otherwise) his death was a case of suicide.

Condorcet's great legacy was his *Progress of the Human Mind*, first published the year after his death. It is generally seen as his primary contribution to social philosophy and to social science. We may, however, mention another of his writings which even now in the early twenty-first century, remains as a contribution to social science. In 1785 he wrote his *Essay on the Application of Analysis to the Probability of Majority Decisions*. This work was clearly mathematical in nature, but it was intended for social science applications. Here he introduced what has become known as "Condorcet's Paradox," the demonstration that majority voting was subject to certain possible inconsistencies. Considering three candidates for an office, A, B, and C, a majority might prefer Candidate A to B; at the same time a majority might prefer B to C, and still another pairing might prefer C to A. This possible lack of consistency posed, in Condorcet's view, a real problem for democratic elections.

Condorcet also worked out a rational method for dealing with such electoral problems. It has become known as the "Condorcet Method," which uses pair-wise comparisons as a key part of voting. It has given rise to several variations discussed by modern theorists of voting procedures. Never mind that no nation today uses elections based directly on the methods Condorcet promoted, his enunciation of the mathematical problems in counting votes are still important in the literature of game theory.[11]

After the Revolution

The French Revolution was one of the great watersheds of Western thought. It had been based on ideals of liberty, equality, and fraternity, in turn seen as expressions of an underlying devotion to human reason and natural law. These ideals did not die with the rise of Napoleon (indeed, Napoleon used them as part of the ideology for his rule) or with the restoration of the monarchy which followed his rule. At the same time, a revulsion against the excesses of the revolution strengthened the resolve of conservatives to resist new ideas. France in particular became a battleground between liberals and conservatives—a split which has continued well beyond the nineteenth century.

There was no doubt about the sympathies of the family into which Auguste Comte was born. They were Roman Catholic and Royalist. Despite the fact that his father was a government employee in the Department of Taxation and thus part of Napoleon's rule, he did everything possible to see that his son would not be contaminated by the radical movements then afoot. In this his success was short-lived.

Born January 19, 1798, in Montpellier, southern France, young Comte soon showed himself to have ideas of his own. He seemed to question everything he was taught. After being educated locally, he went to the prestigious École Polytechnique in Paris to prepare for a career in engineering. Soon, however, his insubordinate spirit caused a change in plans. He led students in petitioning to dismiss an unpopular professor, with the direct result that he and the other students involved were expelled.[12]

Returning to Montpellier in 1816, Comte tried briefly to carry on scholarly activities there; but he found his intellectual ambitions stifled by his conservative parents. Within a year he was back in Paris, seeking to function there as an independent scholar. He supported himself mainly by giving private lessons in mathematics. He became generally known as an able young man of letters, and he translated into French a book written by a British mathematician. He enjoyed the cultural life of Paris and sought recognition within its highest intellectual circles.

One group Comte soon discovered was that which was gathered around Claude-Henri, Comte de Saint-Simon. Saint-Simon, though limited in his formal education, was a man of enormous intellectual interests, and these were shared with a group of followers. He wrote several books on science and sought in the idea of gravitation the basic foundation for all science. Saint-Simon, a brilliant though erratic thinker, then changed his focus to the social sciences and to social reform. His *Reconstruction of European Society* was published in 1816. Soon thereafter he renounced his noble title, began giving away his property, and devoted himself to the ideals of socialism.

In 1817 Comte heard that Saint-Simon was seeking a new secretary. He sought to take advantage of this, and was accepted by the famous writer. He remained working closely with his mentor for six years, writing a good deal of the material that came out under Saint-Simon's name. This included an extended essay on "The Scientific Labors Necessary for the Reorganization of Society," which Saint-Simon published as his own work in 1824. This angered Comte, who abruptly broke off his relationship to Saint-Simon. The elder scholar died the next year and became something of a cult hero among a small group of Christian socialist followers.

Although many of the ideas Comte published in his later works had a remarkable similarity to key themes of Saint-Simon, he avoided mentioning his early mentor as their source. After his break with Saint-Simon, he wrote as though the two had never been associated. Comte was now on his own as an intellectual master.

"The Intellect is My Lord"

In 1826, Comte started a series of lectures in which he intended to cover all the fields of science. These lectures were to become the basis of Comte's most distinguished contribution, *A Course of Positive Philosophy*, published in six volumes from 1830 to 1842. He attempted to cover all fields of human knowledge from a thoroughly scientific perspective. In the "Positivism" which he espoused there was no room for human sentiment. Everything must be factually presented and logically analyzed. All arguments must be purely intellectual, for, as he affirmed, "the intellect is my Lord."[13]

Comte had limited funds at this time and had to live quite frugally. He continued to tutor students, received some payment for his lectures, and served for several years as an external examiner (interviewing candidates for admission from outside of Paris) for the school he had once attended, the École Polytechnique. Despite his limited means, he was able to find a female companion to share his home and help provide household and sexual comforts.

Comte met Caroline Massin on a Paris street in 1821. She had a pleasant smile and seemed eager to hear of his ideas. As she more and more met his practical needs, Comte, in 1825, offered her marriage. This was partly to assure that she would not be regularly seen in the company of another man and to help remove her name from the official listing of Paris prostitutes. Nevertheless, Caroline served her husband well in managing what little money they had and by being a supportive intellectual companion.

She also nurtured him through a mental breakdown in 1827, when he appeared to be unable to function productively for a year and at one time attempted suicide by jumping into the Seine. However, Comte seemed to show little appreciation for, or emotional involvement with, his wife. Several times she left him, with the final departure in 1842. However, they remained officially married, and he continued to send her half his income for as long as he lived.

Comte saw himself as a thoroughgoing rationalist—both in his personal life and in his lectures. He developed personal rituals to clear his mind of all obstructions and less and less paid attention to what anyone else said or wrote. This, he claimed, helped him establish his own command over the fundamental intellectual truths he had to offer.

What Comte saw as his most basic truth became known as the "law of the three stages." This was the notion that all areas of human understanding tended to show a basic progression from mythological to scientific representation. He called the three basic stages of thought the theological, the metaphysical, and the positive. Human thought, both in the history of mankind and in the life of the individual, begins with a series of fictions. They are mythological in nature rather than based on factual knowledge. This is Comte's "theological" stage. From there the progression is toward abstract thinking, where central dogmas form the basis of understanding. This is the "metaphysical" stage. Finally, we arrive at human understanding based on the facts of our own experience and the regularities of these facts. With this rise of scientific thought (during what Comte termed the "positive" stage), comes an ever-growing mastery of the forces around us.

This progression from myth to science forms the background for Comte's *Course of Positive Philosophy*, though he traced his basic insight for this idea back to 1822, when he was still working with Saint-Simon. Regardless of its origin, this "law of the three stages" was clear in its implication that the future must belong to science. There should be no need to continue with philosophies based on rational abstractions. Philosophers must become scientists, grounded in general principles drawn from empirical observation. This is basically what Comte had in mind in his philosophy of "positivism."

Comte's Hierarchy of the Sciences

Not only is there a general progression of the development of human thought, according to Comte, but this progression varies among different fields of knowledge.

He recognized the basic areas of science as mathematics, astronomy, physics, chemistry, biology, and social science. Each of these fields had its sub-fields (for example, he saw psychology as a part of biology and economics as part of social science), but each had its own general laws which must apply also to its sub-fields. The most basic field of all he saw as mathematics, which was the first to become scientific and the foundation for much of the other sciences. Next most basic was astronomy, then physics, then chemistry, and then biology.

Each of these fields of basic science depends on the knowledge of previous fields, so there has been a general progression in their order of developing into fully scientific fields. First, mathematics, next astronomy, then physics, followed by chemistry and biology. In general, the more complex the science, the later was its development. Finally, must come social science, now ready for development into a true science.

In his earlier writings Comte used the term "social physics" to represent his conception of a general social science. Later, in 1839, he coined the term "sociology" to refer to this field. Sociology, in his view, was to become a general science of social phenomena. Since social phenomena were more complex than those of the physical or biological areas, it is not surprising that sociology was the last of the basic sciences to develop. Nevertheless, the time was now ripe for such a science, and Comte was prepared to show the way for it to emerge.

Of central importance was the matter of methods of study which Comte held must be based on careful observation rather than speculation. Science, however, develops not by just collecting an array of facts; the facts must be seen in terms of their most general underlying principles or scientific laws.

Comte saw four main methods for sociology: observation, experiment, comparison, and the historical method. Observation, Comte believed, must be central. He saw the basis of human knowledge in the experience of the senses, for facts must ultimately be derived from what people can see and hear. Facts that can be reported by observers and verified by others must be the basis of any true science. Experiments, as Comte understood them, referred not so much to formal investigations in the laboratory as to the general practice of controlled observation. To make our observations systematically under various conditions was what Comte had in mind here. Comte placed great emphasis on what he called the method of comparison. Different orders of facts could be compared to see what generalizations might combine them in broader terms—as well as to identify key differences. For example, the study of different societies, or of different social classes within the same society, could be used to give us fundamental insights into how human society works. Finally, there was the historical method. The records of the past could be used in place of first-hand observation for many important scientific purposes. History was thus a key part of sociology. Much of the subject matter of this new science could be based on factually based historical studies.

This was the program for research that Comte set forth for his new science of sociology. He also identified the main areas for this field by dividing sociology into social statics and social dynamics. Social statics was the study of actions and reactions within the organization of society. Basically, this was how the social system (which he sometimes saw as similar to biological systems) functioned. Social dynamics, on the other hand, is the study of change, especially historical change. History is here the key method for showing how the human race has changed and advanced.

Comte saw much work to be done to make social statics and social dynamics true fields of science. He freely gave his advice, though he himself provided little research beyond historical observations. Perhaps he felt it sufficient that he had provided the big picture. Most important in his teaching was his law of the three stages, which led to the suggestion that the study of human society was the next field to be developed as a true science.

Positivism Reconsidered

In 1844, at the home of some friends, Comte met a woman he considered breathtakingly beautiful. She was introduced to him as Madame Clotilde de Vaux.

Her blond hair, blue eyes, elegant figure, and modest demeanor struck him almost immediately as representing the feminine ideal. He was soon seeking every opportunity to be in her company. Unfortunately, she was married, as was he; but in both cases the marriage appeared dead. Her husband, by whom she had been deeply disappointed, had not been seen for five years. He had been a local tax official who left his accounts in disarray; and then, rather than face an inspection, just disappeared (with about 15,000 francs).

Considering his general self-confidence, Comte was unusually shy in his early meetings with Clotilde. At first she was not impressed by him personally, despite his great reputation as a scholar. But he persisted. Soon they had formed a close bond of mutual respect. As a writer of some talents herself, Clotilde began to carry on an intimate correspondence with Auguste. Though she remained too modest and reticent to engage in any sexual activity, they soon were involved in a deep love affair. Then she became ill, much more seriously than those around her realized. Within a year of their first meeting, Clotilde was dead from tuberculosis. Comte's grief appeared beyond consolation.

But Comte continued with his scholarly writing. His attention was now directed to the applications of social science for the building of a better world. He maintained his basic philosophy of positivism, but it came through with less rigidity than it had in his *Course of Positive Philosophy*. His new work, *A System of Positive Polity*, was published in four volumes from 1851 to 1854. It was dedicated in loving memory to Clotilde de Vaux.

Comte remains best known for his *Positive Philosophy*, though close scholars of his work often see his *Positive Polity* as the more mature statement of his thinking. The *Polity* seems less rigid in its promotion of positivist philosophy. In part this may be due to its focus on social philosophy. Comte always had seen the science of society as more complex in its subject matter than the other sciences, and the complexities only increased as he sought to show how the insights of sociology might be applied to the task of social reconstruction. In any event, in this later work Comte had more room for the consideration of human sentiments, for he understood that society needs to be based on a consensus that transcends the rational interests of its individuals.

In his final years, Comte became ever more intense in the worship of his beloved Clotilde. He would spend hours each day in rituals to revive his memories of her. His scholarly work declined, though he did continue to do some writing. His last book was his *Subjective Synthesis*, published in 1856. His final contributions were devoted especially to the promotion of a Religion of Humanity. His respect for his Roman Catholic roots had increased in the social conservatism of his last years. Indeed, the religion he suggested, with Humanity itself the object of worship, had a series of sacraments and a priesthood that showed strong similarities to those of the Church he had so clearly rejected in his youth.

Comte's life came to an end in 1857, a victim of cancer. Despite his final work as a supporter of religion, he is usually remembered as a strong, hard-headed proponent of positivism, a philosophy with no room for human sentiment. He is also revered as the father of sociology, for he both gave its name to that field and outlined its primary subject matter. In this regard, however, it is suitable to agree with twentieth-century students of social thought that sociology may be seen as "an inevitable result of the growing conviction that an adequate science of society was a necessity" and a natural "product of a gradually improving method of analyzing social phenomena." It should therefore not be seen as "the fortuitous and questionable invention of one man, nor the perishable and exotic ideology of a brief period in the history of Western Europe." That may well be, but it is still true that Comte was the person who first gave this new science explicit recognition, and he did so with full consciousness of the legacy of the Age of Enlightenment.[14]

Rationality and Nonrationality

The coming of social science, illustrated by such early proponents as Condorcet and Comte, was primarily an application of the highest standards of rationality to the analysis of human society. Both of these thinkers were products of the Enlightenment, when human reason became the basis of all judgments. Social science clearly had its origins in this search for how rationality can best be applied to the world of human society. Both Condorcet and Comte saw this as a new task for science.

Another, though less obvious, similarity of Condorcet and Comte was in the way they illustrated the power of sentiments which went beyond reason. There appears something unreasonable about the zeal with which Condorcet, a fugitive during the most violent days of the French Revolution, so confidently predicted mankind's future progress. Here was expressed as much faith as reason. Likewise was the case with Comte. Despite his reputation as the complete rationalist, he ended his years in promoting a new religion which was as much based on the heart as the head.

The subsequent history of social science has continued an ambivalent devotion to rationality. Empirical evidence and systematic rationality must be the primary means of trying to understand human society; this remains as the central theme for social science. But there is also the recognition that human identities are involved and that humans are moved deeply by sentiments as well as by facts. Further, the search for a better world, a central purpose for those who desire to apply science to the study of society, raises questions about the values which may be involved. Not all of these values can be neatly summarized by principles of rationality.

2

The Three Bases of Social Science

The Social Sciences and Social Science

Social science today is usually seen as a series of academic disciplines between the natural sciences and the humanities. There are, on the one hand, the physical and biological sciences, plus mathematics. On the other hand we have the fields of languages, literature, philosophy, and the arts. Somewhere between are such fields as sociology, political science, and economics. We call these fields—with legacies both in the natural sciences and the humanities but with their own distinctive pursuits as well—the "social sciences."

Any contemporary enumeration of the social sciences must include economics, political science, and sociology. Of these, economics was the first to become a recognized discipline, though it was often called "political economy" in the nineteenth century. In any case, as a central body of thought it can be traced as far back as 1776, when Adam Smith published *The Wealth of Nations*. By the early twentieth century, it was widely recognized as the systematic study of the production, distribution, and consumption of goods and services, with market analysis a central theme. By the end of the century, its subject matter was less clearly defined, though it was still recognized as a discipline dealing with decisions (by individuals or by collectives) within the framework of systems of exchange.

Sociology emerged out of social philosophy during the last half of the nineteenth century. We have seen that its name was coined by Auguste Comte, setting it forth as the general science of society. Early in the twentieth century, its ambitions were slightly reduced, as it gave room for other disciplines to share the burdens of studying the increasing complexities of human communities. What remained as its central focus by the end of the century was the study of how groups are organized into society ("social structure") and how changes take place in society ("social change").

17

Political science emerged gradually out of political philosophy during the nineteenth century. By the early part of the twentieth century, there was a body of knowledge about the behavior of people in governmental contexts which supplemented the more general ideas of theorists. This combination became recognized as one of the central social science disciplines, political science. By the end of the century, it sometimes became conceptualized more broadly and theoretically as the study of power in human society, though the main subject matter of political scientists remained with matters such as governmental structures, political parties, and international relations.

Psychology must also be mentioned among the social sciences, though clearly it has roots in biology as well as in the study of human social behavior. Scientific traditions began in German laboratories during the last half of the nineteenth century, and by 1890, when William James published *The Principles of Psychology*, the field had become a recognized scientific discipline. Clearly it involved social as well as biological subject matter. Soon the social content of psychology was made the focus of a special field of study, and thus social psychology was born. Social psychologists came out of both psychology and sociology, and the first textbooks of this new field began being published early in the twentieth century. Meanwhile, academic psychology during the twentieth century moved from being the study of "mind" to become the "science of behavior." Behavior, of course, has its roots in physiological processes, but it must also be seen within the context of social stimuli. The boundary line between social psychology (focusing on social behavior) and the rest of psychology became more and more blurred during the twentieth century, just as was the case of that between social psychology (focusing on direct interaction between individuals) and the rest of sociology.

Anthropology, the study of humans in all their forms, is also generally recognized as a social science. As with psychology, its roots extend into biology as well as social phenomena. The systematic study of cultures began in the last half of the nineteenth century, and these studies became the basis of ethnology or cultural anthropology. Physical anthropology (the study of human physical forms) and archeology (the study of remains from the past) represent other forms of anthropology, though these have not always been clearly distinct from cultural anthropology.

Then there is, and always has been, history. Historical data are part of all the social sciences. Comte, in fact, treated it as the base for most generalizations in his new science of social life. But history as a recognized discipline (focused on written records of the human past) has always been seen as partly in the humanities as well as among the social sciences. The great works of philosophy, literature, and the arts have all been pursued in part through historical writings. But historians since the time of Thucydides (who wrote more than twenty-four centuries ago) have also included social and political analyses in their works. Only in the twentieth century, however, has "social history" (based on the historical treatment of selected aspects of society) come to have a major place within the discipline of history.

Economics, sociology, political science, psychology, anthropology, and history became disciplines through their recognition by institutions of higher education. Universities have long been organized into departments, and advanced training is guided by the faculty of a particular academic department. In this manner, we have seen the rise of social science disciplines. As fields became recognized as departments (not just courses) in more and more universities, they gradually came to be seen as the basic social science disciplines. Of course, the process of differentiation did not stop with these six disciplines. Each of them also became divided into smaller fields, some of which—such as demography (the study of population) or criminology (the study of crime and punishment)—often became departments, and thereby recognized as disciplines with their own identities. Also there have developed numerous applied fields (from business administration, to early child education, to social work), and these typically see themselves as disciplines which draw from a variety of social science fields. Social science has become today much more diversified than the basic science envisaged by Auguste Comte in the nineteenth century.

Most social scientists today identify themselves with one of the disciplines we have mentioned. They see themselves as economists, sociologists, political scientists, psychologists, anthropologists, or historians. But often their work points beyond their disciplinary boundaries. There is still room for a broad-based science of social phenomena, whatever may be the disciplines claimed by those scholars involved.

Upon what does a unity of social science rest? Whatever the particular field, there are several broad activities which must be pursued if social science is to succeed in its work. We can identify the following three primary bases for social science: the empirical base, the theoretical base, and the pragmatic base. The rest of this book will be organized around these three foundations of social science work.

The Empirical Base

The empirical base for social science consists of observations of the social scientist, or records of observations made by others. These are the data for analysis, the "findings" in research reports, the facts upon which generalizations are to be made.

There are a variety of methods of research in the social sciences. Sometimes direct observation is the method of choice. Sometimes survey research is used. Sometimes it is possible to control the variables sufficiently well to conduct an experiment. Often data gathered by others—previous compilations, such as census data, historical records, and other forms of accumulated information—are used. In any event, the data must be available for verification by others. It must be reported in such a way that main findings may be confirmed by others, for it is only through the accumulation of verified knowledge that a science may grow. Sometimes this verification is easier when findings are expressed in the language of mathematics, though qualitative as well as quantitative research remains important for the social sciences.

The Theoretical Base

The theoretical base of social science consists of the thoughtful analyses applied to the data being considered. Findings do not speak for themselves, but must be interpreted in terms of broader generalizations.

The work of theory is to make logical inferences from, and to show wider meanings of, whatever data may be at hand. Sometimes this takes the form of a general conceptual scheme, into which various kinds of observations may be included. Sometimes it takes the form of a mathematical model to represent a given phenomenon in abstract form. In any event, the work of theory—just as is the case for the work of research—must be presented to other social scientists in such a way that it can be critically evaluated. For it is only through the consensus of those in a field of science that its general assumptions and propositions can be accepted as valid.

The Pragmatic Base

The utility of the social sciences (just as is the case with other fields of science) provides another foundation for work in these fields. There is always a broader audience, largely motivated by very practical concerns, which must show interest if a field of science is to survive and prosper.

Sometimes applications of the social sciences may be quite specific. Examples may include the way the idea of a representative sample has moved from survey research in sociology to becoming a mainstay in market research, the manner with which the economists' concept of gross domestic product has became a key concern for the formulation of public policies, or the way conditioning procedures of psychology have been applied to the treatment of young delinquents. With a wide array of such practical contributions are social scientists able to justify their work to the public at large.

But there is also a more general function of the social sciences in providing a critical eye for looking at the society around us. This often leads to suggesting how changes might be made to improve the general framework of social life. To such pioneers as Condorcet and Comte this was a key part of their work, and it remains today important for justifying the work of social scientists. For better or worse, social scientists are part of their societies, and their insights can be used in the efforts of a society to seek its improvement. Social science thus has its social reformers as well as its researchers and theorists.

So we have our social science researchers, theorists, and social reformers. Often, we should also note, a combination of these bases of the work of social science will be found emphasized by the efforts of a particular social scientist.

The Masters

The point that we have just made—that the work of a social scientist frequently combines more than one of the three bases we have mentioned—seems especially true of those who might be called "masters" of social science. We refer here to the work of social scientists who have become especially well known for their contributions.

Who are these "masters"? For the last half of the nineteenth century we may consider such individuals as Karl Marx and Herbert Spencer in such a category. As we move into the twentieth century many more names come to mind.[1]

What other figures in social science deserve to be called "masters," as we move into the twentieth century? The lists here could include many names.

The eleven social scientists whose lives and works we choose to treat in the rest of this book certainly are not the only candidates of the twentieth century worth considering. We have selected them largely because they help us illustrate what we have called the three bases of social science. Some rather directly show the empirical spirit, some are primarily theorists, and some seem to express more clearly a pragmatic bent. All of them, however, have significantly influenced the nature of social science as it has come to exist in the opening years of the twenty-first century.

Part 2

Discoverers

3

Louis and Mary Leakey
and the Dawn of Humanity

Beginnings

Louis Leakey's childhood was spent mostly in Kenya, where his parents were Anglican missionaries. He was born on August 7, 1903, at their mission station, which was little more than a clearing in the forest north of Naroibi. In this area he spent most of his childhood—among the plants and wild animals found along narrow forest paths and with native Kikuyu as his friends. Although he began his formal schooling in England, Louis returned to Africa in 1913, and the onset of World War I kept the Leakey family there until 1919. During these years, Louis came of age among the Kikuyu, actually becoming initiated into the tribe. He later recalled that "in language and in mental outlook I was more Kikuyu than English, and it never occurred to me to act other than Kikuyu."[1]

Louis found it difficult to adjust to secondary education in Great Britain. He made few friends among his English schoolmates. However, he studied hard and was admitted to Cambridge University, where he left an impression as a free-wheeling but able young man. He concentrated his studies in prehistory. Before completing his undergraduate studies he joined a dinosaur fossil hunting expedition to eastern Africa, then returned to Cambridge to graduate with top honors in 1926. He was soon awarded a fellowship to lead his own archeological expedition to East Africa.

Among visitors to the excavations Louis made in Kenya was a bright young former student at Cambridge who was impressed by his originality and range of knowledge. Impulsively, and almost immediately, Louis suggested marriage. Although they were not married just then, their romance continued through long distance correspondence, and Louis and Frida Leakey were married in the summer of 1928. Soon she accompanied him on a new East African archaeological expedition.

For several years Louis divided his time between work in Kenya and further studies and writing at Cambridge. He was awarded the doctoral degree in 1930 and his first book, *The Stone Age Cultures of Kenya Colony*, was published the following year. In 1931 Louis and Frida also had their first child, and later that year Louis was off on another expedition to Africa. This time he made Olduvai Gorge, on the edge of the Serengeti Plain just south of Kenya, the focus of his attentions. Soon his wife and daughter came to share the excitement of what Louis was discovering there. Although he found no human bones (an earlier human discovery there by a German before the war had helped attract him to Olduvai), the beds there were rich in early fossils.

Louis also explored other sites in East Africa. At one of them, Kanjera, on the shore of Lake Victoria, Louis and his crew found small pieces of a human skull; and at nearby Kanam they uncovered a piece of a human jawbone. He carried his samples of Kanjera Man and Kanam Man back to England to support his claim that *Homo sapiens* had been present in East Africa for many thousands of years.

Louis and Frida then established a home near Cambridge, where Louis now had teaching duties. Another child was on the way in 1933 when Louis met a young woman named Mary Nicol, with whom he pursued a whirlwind courtship. Louis and Mary then confronted Frida with their desire for marriage. Frida, though devastated, decided not to stand in their way.[2]

Mary Douglas Nicol had been the daughter of a landscape painter who spent much of his time traveling and painting in France, Italy, and Egypt. He returned to England mainly to sell his pictures, and it was in England that Erskine and Cecilia Nicol had their only child, Mary, born on February 6, 1913.

Mary spent much of her childhood in France, where she showed a strong interest in archeology. Close to her father, she also developed her artistic talents. She had little formal education, reacting so strongly against the strains of school discipline that, after she was expelled from two schools, her parents did not insist that she continue formal studies.

After her father's death in 1926, Mary and her mother returned to England. There she audited college courses in archeology and joined several archeological digs. She also worked as an artist, providing illustrations for some of the archeological reports.

Soon after he met her, Louis Leakey arranged for Mary to work on illustrations for the book he was then writing, *Adam's Ancestors*. Their romance blossomed quickly. Mary's mother was horrified at this quick turn in events, but Louis and Mary were resolved to pursue their affair wherever it might lead.

Despite his marriage to another woman, Louis and Mary spent much of 1935 traveling together in Africa. When they returned to England, their scandal prevented a renewal of the research fellowship Louis had held at Cambridge University. Soon Louis was officially divorced, and he and Mary were then free to marry.

Louis and Mary Leakey confirmed their personal partnership on December 24, 1936, in a simple ceremony in an English registry office. Only three friends or relatives were present. Mary's mother and an aunt were there—reluctantly, for they had opposed the match—and Louis had no family members present. His parents did not even know about his relationship with Mary, despite the fact that the two had been living together for more than a year. With Louis at the wedding was only a boyhood friend from the Kikuyu tribe of East Africa who happened to be visiting England at the time.

The month after their wedding Louis and Mary left for Africa, where both would spend most of the rest of their lives unearthing remains of the human past.

In Africa

Africa was just then being considered as a possible home continent for early man. Raymond Dart's South African discovery of *Australopithecus*, first reported in 1924, was still a subject of controversy. Some doubted whether these bones represented the human branch among the primates. Many scholars still felt more comfortable with a European or Asian location for early human evolution. Louis Leakey was among only a small number of scientists who then saw East Africa as the most promising place to search for human origins.

Paleoanthroplogy was clearly Louis Leakey's first love, and he devoted enormous energies in trying to find funding for his East African excavations. But he had a wide range of other interests as well. He served in intelligence work in East Africa during World War II, and he continued doing amateur detective work for the colonial administration for years afterward. A distinguished naturalist, he served for many years as curator of a museum in Nairobi, which eventually grew (especially later under the leadership of his son Richard) to became Kenya's National Museums. As a cultural anthropologist, he studied extensively East African tribal societies, with a special interest in his own Kikuyu tribe. In fact, when he and Mary went back to Africa shortly after their marriage, his support was primarily from a grant to do a systematic study of the Kikuyu. He continued this project throughout the rest of his life. However, despite his numerous books, the main results of his Kikuyu studies were still unpublished at the time of his death in 1972.

Though working primarily as a field archeologist, Mary Leakey also had other important interests, especially the study of African rock paintings. Some of these prehistoric works rivaled the talent shown by the European cave artists. In 1983, she was pleased to see her book on this work, *Africa's Vanishing Art*, finally published.

So both Louis and Mary Leakey had other interests beyond archeology and paleontology. Still, their search to uncover the story of early man was for both clearly the center of their lives. They dug at a number of promising sites in the area around Nairobi, Kenya, but none attracted their attention as much as did the Olduvai Gorge location.

At the Gorge

The Olduvai Gorge was actually a junction of two badly eroded depressions near the edge of Africa's Great Rift Valley in what is now northern Tanzania. Although an area of wild beauty near high mountains and at the edge of the Serengeti Plains, Olduvai had no established roads to connect the area with East African cities, and living conditions at the site were extremely primitive. Still, Louis and Mary Leakey returned to Olduvai year after year, making it almost as much their home as was their house in Nairobi.

Olduvai yielded a rich variety of stone tools, many of which were estimated by geological evidence as being left more than a million years ago. Also found there were many bones of extinct animals. However, before 1959, no clearly human bones were found at Olduvai by the Leakeys, despite their enormous efforts.

Fragments of a relatively complete skull of an ancient ape were found by Mary in 1948 on Rusinga Island near the eastern shore of Lake Victoria. This individual, who lived more than 15 million years ago, was named *Proconsul*, and there was a widely publicized debate regarding whether this might represent a form ancestral to both modern apes and humans. At any rate, *Proconsul* brought worldwide attention to the work of the Leakeys, which helped them receive modest funding for their excavations at Olduvai and elsewhere in eastern Africa.

Then, in July of 1959, Olduvai finally yielded a major discovery of human-like, or hominid, bones. First just a tooth was found; then Mary came across what appeared to be a major part of a skull. She waited for a scheduled arrival of a naturalist film crew (creating an "On Safari" series) before carefully unearthing the skull in front of the cameras. This provided quite a dramatic impact, for it was the first large skull of an early hominid unearthed in East Africa. Louis Leakey named this apparently new species *Zinjanthropus*, though later it became considered as a special form of *Australopithicus* that lived about 1.75 million years ago. (Early human-like forms have generally come to be placed either under the genus *Australopithicus*, including most of the earlier forms, or the genus *Homo*, including most later forms.)

Whatever the final interpretation of their find, the Leakeys' work now became world famous. After almost three decades of systematic work there, Olduvai Gorge now became one of the best-known places in all of Africa. New sources of funding (especially from America's National Geographic Society) became available to expand greatly the Olduvai operations, and within a few years tourists began to find their way to this remote part of Africa.

Louis and Mary Leakey had three children. These sons—Jonathan, Richard, and Philip—became integral parts of the Olduvai crew. In fact, it was Jonathan who first found the bone fragments of another hominid only a year after the discovery of "Zinj." Much closer in form to modern humans, these new bones also seemed to be associated with simple stone tools. Louis (following the suggestion of Raymond Dart, who had originally discovered australopithecines in South Africa) called this new species *Homo habilis*. "Handy Man" is what the popular press soon called this new form because its hand bones suggested an increased facility for grasping objects.

The designation of this find as *Homo* was for a time quite controversial. No other well-identified forms of that genus had been found who lived that long ago—roughly at the same time as Zinj. Part of the controversy concerned cranial capacity, for Handy Man had only a slightly larger brain than that shown by australopithecine skulls. It was clearly smaller than the other early *Homo* finds which had by then been unearthed elsewhere (generally given the designation of *Homo erectus*). However, as other discoveries similar to Handy Man were made, paleontologists slowly came to accept *Homo habilis* as the earliest identifiable form of the *Homo* line. Louis felt vindicated, for he long had emphasized that the very earliest forms of true human beings were to be found in East Africa.

Jonathan's brother Philip, while only twelve years old, took charge of a small project at Olduvai during his Christmas vacation. This led to the excavation of the earliest known structure built for human habitation. But of the three sons, it was Richard who made the biggest name for himself in paleoanthropology. This was despite the fact that he early promised himself that he would *not* become an archeologist. Still, he came to take over from his father an important leadership position at the museum in Nairobi when only twenty-three years of age, and he began to lead his own expeditions (which eventually became even larger and more systematically organized than those of his father) shortly thereafter.

In 1968, Richard began explorations along the eastern shore of Lake Turkana, where he found important australopithecine materials. These small-brained creatures, living about 1.7 million years ago, already had a fully bipedal posture. Later, in 1972, the same area yielded the best preserved skull of any *Homo* form in East Africa. This find became known as "1470" (after its museum identification number). It differed in small ways from other *Homo* finds from its time (about 1.85 million years ago), leading to the question of whether or not there were at least two different species of the *Homo* genus living in Africa at the same time. This possibility was further supported when Richard's crew found a nearly complete *Homo erectus* skeleton in the Lake Turkana area.

Celebrities

After the dramatic hominid finds by the Leakeys in 1959 and 1960, Louis became a world celebrity and spent much of his time traveling over the globe to promote the East African work.

Louis was a great salesman for the Leakey research efforts—not only for the search for early man but also for other primate studies. Despite great success in fund raising, he constantly had a wider variety of projects than he was able to manage. Then there was the hectic pace of his speaking tours. A very popular speaker, he basked in the spotlight of the lecture hall and was particularly charming with smaller groups. This helped greatly to promote his East African studies, but it also kept him away from spending much time in painstaking field work.

Mary took over the project at Olduvai, organizing the excavations and leading her crews with a firm hand. Her group made few dramatic discoveries but added immensely to our knowledge of human prehistory. When she came to publish her findings on the earliest layers at Olduvai, she provided data on more than 37,000 artifacts, twenty fossilized human bones, and the remains of many more animals. Here was indeed a treasure-trove for the study of African human life extending back to nearly two million years ago.[3]

Louis and Mary led essentially separate lives during their last few years. A heart attack led to Louis' death in London on October 1, 1972. He had just finished the second volume of his autobiography and was preparing for another speaking tour in the United States. In her own autobiography, Mary recalls:

> I had to watch Louis decline from the height of his intellectual powers and the fullness of his charm, to become irritable and irrational, someone for whom his colleagues had quite frequently to cover up, out of respect for what had once been.

Mary regretted that she felt "powerless to bring him any help or comfort or support," leaving him to feel that "I too had changed, had become cold and uncaring, had abandoned him when he needed me most."[4]

The Search Continues

About twenty miles from Olduvai was another site, Laetoli, that proved to be extremely productive. It was at Laetoli in the late 1970s that Mary Leakey and her associates discovered a variety of animal tracks. These were preserved by unusual conditions that had encrusted a moist layer of volcanic ash.

One day in 1978 a member of the Laetoli team started to hammer a rock to bits, only to discover that it included a human heel print. Further study identified a long trail of footprints left by at least two individuals, one of them with an unusually large foot. This brought forth a special mystery. The print was left under the ash about 3.6 million years ago, and by the size of the large foot the larger hominid must have been about six feet tall. But all previous hominid remains from that long ago had been much smaller than that. How did these individuals fit into the classifications of early humans? This question brought forth a great deal of debate when the discoveries were described for the scientific world the following year.

What was not in dispute was that the footprints demonstrated that early hominids had feet much like our own, and apparently used them in much the same way—well over three million years ago. This tended to support the idea that an upright posture, rather than a large brain, was the chief factor separating early man from other primates. The brain size of these very early forms of humanity was only about 430 cubic centimeters—very close to the cranial capacities of today's African apes. But their footprints were of the kind that might have been left by fully modern humans.

One day in 1982 Mary Leakey awoke to find that she could not see out of her left eye. The medical examination that followed concluded that she had suffered from a thrombosis which had permanently damaged her eye. She was then still living at her Olduvai camp, but she soon decided that it was time to move back to Nairobi. In the following year she established herself back in the home where she and Louis lived during most of the time when they were away from Olduvai. Here she continued her archeological analyses, and from here she traveled to receive formal recognition for her work from all over the world.

Before her death in 1996, Mary Leakey observed a great deal of controversy over the interpretation of the early African hominid discoveries which had been made by Louis, herself, her son Richard, and by an increasing array of other paleontologists. In general, she tried to steer clear of strong opinions about the specific paths of human evolution. Much more was it her style to focus upon what had actually been found at the various sites. In the final comments of her autobiography, she expressed herself in this way:

> Many of my colleagues expend a great deal of time and mental energy in reconstructing trees of hominid evolution. They juggle with Miocene apes, the various australopithecines, and with types of early *Homo*, sometimes making a simple evolutionary pattern and sometimes ones that are extremely complex. It is good fun, and an entertaining pastime if not taken too seriously, but in the present state of our knowledge I do not believe it is possible to fit the known hominid fossils into a reliable pattern.

She concludes that "For the present we would do well to concentrate on discovering new, firmly dated specimens and spend less time in putting forward our own, personal interpretations."[5]

The Context of Discovery

Great discoveries in the social sciences involve skill, perseverance, and luck. These were all present in the work of the Leakeys during their discovery of early human remains in Africa. Louis Leakey had a variety of skills essential for their work, and Mary quickly developed an outstanding ability for archeological investigation. Their perseverance is legendary; year after year they continued their work at Olduvai even though breakthroughs were slow in coming. And they had the good fortune, from time to time, to look at just the right place to uncover key evidence about early man.

But more than great discoverers are involved in great discoveries. There is also the larger context of scientific work within which the discoveries must find their place.

An important point to note is that discoverers usually operate in teams. A few bits of fossilized human bone might be picked up by just walking over the land, but such finds are rare. Most evidences of early humans found by the Leakeys came through organized excavations. These involved well managed camps of scientists and African workers digging day after day for new fossils or artifacts, then systematically documenting whatever was unearthed.

There is also a larger public whose interest and support are vital. Louis Leakey was a master communicator when it came to describing the significance of their discoveries to eager listeners and readers from all over the world. And he was persuasive in convincing funding agencies to continue fieldwork support.

Finally, there is the community of scientific specialists, whose acceptance marks the success of discoveries. The evaluations of other scientists are the ultimate test for works of scientific discovery.

How all of the above factors facilitate and confirm scientific discovery is well illustrated in most of the work of Louis and Mary Leakey. However, the Leakeys also can serve to illustrate how the work of discovery may be hindered when all of these factors are not present.

In 1931 Louis had found a hominid jawbone at Kanam, near the Kenyan shore of Lake Victoria, and a few miles away, at Kanjera, he had found bits of a human skull. He brought these back to England, claiming them as direct evidence of early man in Africa. The Kanam find, in particular, was the object of a great deal of attention, and Louis responded by naming this as a new species, *Homo kanamensis*. By using the *Homo* genus, he suggested that this might be the earliest example yet found of fully human bones.

A great deal of uncertainty remained about the dating of Kanam Man. A piece of bone could tell little, given the dating techniques then available. What was needed was geological evidence from the actual site where the bone had been found. Therefore, when Louis and Mary led their African expedition in the fall of 1934, a reexamination of the Kanam and Kanjera sites was high among their priorities. One of the foremost British geologists, P.G.H. Boswell, was scheduled for a visit soon after their arrival in Kenya to help evaluate the Kanam and Kanjera finds. Unfortunately, when Louis returned to the sites of his discoveries, he found his marking stakes had all vanished—apparently put to use by natives for fishing spears. He could therefore not identify exactly where any of his finds had come from. Although he had made photographs, his main roll of film had come out blank. One of the other members of the party had a photograph of the Kanam site, but this location could not easily be found—and when it was finally located it was not where

Louis remembered finding the jawbone. In brief, Louis had only vague recollections to identify where his bone pieces had been found.

Professor Boswell came and was not impressed. Louis, he found, "was forever darting like a bee, from one new site to another" and unable to give a consistent story of where the finds at either Kanam or Kanjera had been made. Boswell left feeling he had wasted two months of his time. Back in England, he concluded that "the geological age of the mandible and skull fragments is uncertain" and that neither Kanam Man nor Kanjera Man could be properly authenticated. To the dismay of Louis Leakey, many experts who had been so impressed when he had shown them his Kanam and Kanjera pieces, now came to question the value of these discoveries. Some even expressed doubts about Louis' professional competence. As a result, the Leakeys found it much harder for them to get British funding for future work in Africa, and they had to be especially careful in giving detailed reports of their further discoveries.[6]

In their work from that time on, Louis and Mary Leakey did a thorough job of documenting all their discoveries. Gradually the Kanam and Kanjera issues were forgotten, as new evidence of early man in Africa came forth. The Leakeys had well learned their lesson that early human forms do not speak for themselves. Rather, they must be carefully considered in relation to the context in which they are found, and evaluated in the context of the community of knowledgeable scientists in terms of evidence very carefully presented.

4

Margaret Mead
and the Varieties of Human Culture

Margaret Discovers Anthropology

Margaret Mead took only one anthropology course during her four years of college, but that, during her senior year, was enough to convince her that anthropology was her calling. Until then she had sampled widely the fields of knowledge. When she came to Barnard College (part of Columbia University) at eighteen years of age she thought of becoming a creative writer. But gradually her interests changed, and she decided upon psychology as her major field. Then in her final year she took an anthropology course with Franz Boas.[1]

Franz Boas was then leading a new movement in anthropology. The field had started as a series of observations by explorers, missionaries, and other travelers who reported on the strange practices found in the various corners of the world. Then in the last part of the nineteenth century it developed into an academic discipline, organized largely by general theories of human social evolution. When Boas became an anthropologist (after a Ph.D. in physics), he was highly critical of the theorizing then characteristic of the field. He felt that anthropology needed to pay more attention to descriptions of people in their various settings, and to avoid broad generalizations about social evolution. What was needed above all was careful, scientifically organized fieldwork to study human cultural variations. This was the image of anthropology that Boas brought to Margaret Mead, and she was soon convinced that in such work lay her future career. In the end, it was Ruth Benedict (then Boas's assistant, but who was to become Margaret's lifelong friend) who convinced her that she could make her greatest impact as an anthropologist.

Margaret already knew a great deal about the social sciences. From the moment of her birth on December 16, 1901, she was surrounded by social scientists. Her father was a professor in the Wharton School of

Finance and Commerce of the University of Pennsylvania. When Margaret was born, her mother was pursuing a master's degree in sociology and conducting a study of Italian immigrants in southern New Jersey. Influenced especially by her mother, Margaret early became familiar with the cultural differences among Americans. In fact, when she herself wrote her master's thesis ("Intelligence Tests of Italian and American Children") she used the same Italian study group that her mother had identified years earlier. Her results tended to confirm the suspicion of Boas (now her major advisor) that social environments can have a major effect upon what psychologists study as "intelligence."

Margaret responded eagerly to a childhood of rich experience. Her parents put less emphasis on schooling than more direct forms of learning. Her mother arranged for her to have special teachers in a variety of subjects and practical skills. Later she was to recall this kind of education as an especially fitting background for handling anthropological fieldwork.

Margaret seemed especially sensitive to personality differences. Although her father sometimes seemed aloof, his mother, Margaret's grandmother, strongly encouraged an early interest in personality differences, including those within her family. Margaret's mother, when her last child was born in 1911, entered a deep depression, and Margaret, as the oldest child, took on briefly a role of special responsibility within her family. At about the same time, she became an avid reader, spending many hours of her private time reading books.

Her freshman year in college was spent at DePauw University in Indiana (which had been her father's school), but she felt that she did not fit in well there. More at home was she in the cosmopolitan atmosphere of Barnard College, where she became recognized as a spirited intellectual. The Ash Can Cats was the name chosen by an especially talented group of young radicals at Barnard, and Margaret was a central member of this informal group. These women were to remain close friends throughout her life.

A brief interruption in her plans came with Margaret's marriage in 1923 to Luther Cressman, a theological student preparing for—and beginning to practice—the Episcopalian ministry. This followed an engagement of several years, for the two had met at a high school prom in 1917 and soon secretly pledged themselves to marriage.

Then Luther went off to war, and Margaret continued her studies until she finally considered herself ready to become a minister's wife. A bit of a stir was created when she decided to keep her maiden name, but Margaret and Luther began their married life in a small apartment in Manhattan—from where he had to travel by subway to a pastorate in Brooklyn. She later recalled their year together as a peaceful time, though she apparently early found the relationship not to her complete satisfaction. In any event, they ceased living together in 1924, though it would be four years later that Margaret (by then involved with another man) would seek an official divorce. It is ironic that Margaret's new love then, Reo Fortune, was an anthropologist, and that Luther himself was to become an anthropologist.

By the fall of 1924, Margaret was eager for to embark on anthropological fieldwork. She wanted to prove herself as a worthy student of Franz Boas and Ruth Benedict. But where would she go?

Boas suggested that she focus on the study of adolescence in some tribal society, possibly (considering her rather frail appearance—short in stature and less than 100 pounds) close to home among the American Indians. But Margaret preferred to seek out a society that would be more distant and less known, such as in Polynesia. There was an urgency to study these island cultures before they became submerged in the modern world. After some delicate negotiations (in which her father's offer of funding for the trip helped make Polynesia possible) she was on her way to Samoa.

Samoa

Margaret Mead arrived in Pago Pago, the chief city of American Samoa, on August 31, 1925. This followed a stopover of two weeks in Honolulu, where she attempted to immerse herself in whatever materials she could find on Polynesian language and culture. In Samoa, she first stayed in a Pago Pago hotel, especially concentrating on a study of Samoan language. Then she arranged to live with a local chief for ten days in a village away from the city. Here she began to live by Samoan customs and Samoan food.

On November 9 she finally arrived on the remote island of Ta'u (in the Manu'a group about eighty miles east of Pago Pago). This was to be the primary site of her Samoan research efforts. She established living quarters with the only Western household on the island, that of a U.S. Navy chief pharmacist's mate, occupying half of his back porch for her quarters. There she could write her research notes in privacy, but she could also bring her Samoan guests there, individually or in groups. From there she wandered freely about the village, speaking her best Samoan, and making the acquaintance of as many Samoan girls as she could. In this she was given special help by a young woman recommended by the local Christian pastor.

Mead had received almost no training in ethnographic methods before she went to Samoa. Anthropologists were just beginning to discuss the details of field methodology, and Mead's most relevant education came more from her broad general background than from anthropological course work. Her work in psychology was especially helpful for her study of adolescent girls, but she had to invent her own particular applications. Very carefully taking notes on all her experiences, she gradually taught herself the essentials of anthropological fieldwork. The approach she devised was later to be identified as "participant observation," involving the observer fully in the life of the group being studied. Later describing how she went about her work, Mead recalled:

> The adolescent girls, and later the smaller girls whom I found I had also to study, came and filled my screen-room day after day and night after night. Later I borrowed a schoolhouse to give "examinations," and under that heading I was able to give a few simple tests and interview each girl alone. Away from the dispensary I could wander freely about the village or go on fishing trips or stop at a house where a woman was weaving. Gradually I built up a census of the whole village and worked out the background of each of the girls I was studying.

In such a manner she put herself into Samoan life as fully as possible for the approximately six months that she lived on the island of Ta'u. The result was not so much the discovery of this or that specific fact (though Mead carefully preserved her field notes as records of what she found), but rather what general patterns might emerge. Gradually the outlines of what it means to be an adolescent girl in Samoa became understood by Margaret Mead.[2]

Adolescence in Samoa, Mead observed, is not the period of high tension and stress that it generally seems to be in America. In Samoa there appears less of a break between early childhood and adolescence, and also a greater continuity between adolescence and adulthood. At a very early age, by the time most Americans are starting school, Samoan girls are given major responsibilities for their households, including taking care of younger children. So, in one sense, adult responsibilities begin long before puberty. There are no major changes in one's place in society with the onset of puberty. The development of sexuality during adolescence seems easy and natural. It does not appear to be fraught with identity questions or with an ambiguous relation to adult authority. Rather, there is a great deal of freedom among adolescent girls and a gradual progression into adulthood.

After she returned to New York, Mead put into writing the results of her fieldwork. Actually, there were three related writing projects to occupy her attention. There was her doctoral dissertation, "An Inquiry into the Question of Cultural Stability in Polynesia." Not based directly on her fieldwork, this drew mostly upon what other anthropologists had reported about Polynesia. There was also a general report on Samoa, "Social Organization of Manu'a," written with considerable help from Ruth Benedict. This general anthropological monograph had not been expected by Franz Boas, who had suggested that Mead limit her attention to questions about adolescence, but she was eager to prove her mettle as a budding anthropologist. Then there was the report on Samoan adolescence. She chose to write this in the form of a book that might have a wider audience than fellow anthropologists. The manuscript which resulted was, after one rejection from another publisher, submitted to William Morrow, who had just opened his own publishing company.

Morrow was impressed with what Mead had submitted. Here was a very well-written manuscript, vivid in its descriptions of Samoan life, and with clear implications for questions about adolescence more generally. He thought it just might appeal to a general audience, but to enhance this he suggested that she add some material which related more directly to American culture. Mead then added the two final chapters of her book ("Our Educational Problems in the Light of Samoan Contrasts" and "Education for Choice") and it was ready for publication. *Coming of Age in Samoa* was finally published in 1928.[3]

Coming of Age was an immediate publishing success. Readers found Mead's descriptions of Samoa (especially her brief chapter on "A Day in Samoa") enchanting, and many found the implications for America thoughtfully presented. We must, she insisted, use knowledge of other societies as we ponder how we can make our own educational system more responsive to basic human needs. Her mentor Franz Boas was also impressed, for this book supported well his own views about cultural relativity. As he concluded in his foreword:

> The results of her painstaking investigation confirm the suspicion long held by anthropologists, that much of what we ascribe to human nature is no more than a reaction to the restraints put upon us by our civilization.

This general theme of the importance of cultural variations was then just beginning to become a leading part of America's intellectual landscape. This was very much enhanced by what Mead had to say in *Coming of Age*. In addition to its general public appeal, this book became a common requirement in college social science courses. Mead was to become the most famous anthropologist of the twentieth century. She wrote many more books, but none attained the readership of this first one.[4]

From New Guinea to Bali

Although her marriage to Luther Cressman had cooled, Margaret planned to meet him in France on her return trip to the United States. He would then be completing a special fellowship for study abroad and could meet her ship at Marseilles. They then were to travel together in Europe before each would return separately to the United States—with their longer future together still uncertain.

However, Mead's life was sharply altered in the early summer of 1926 on her way from Australia to France aboard the *SS Chitral*. During this voyage of seven weeks she formed a close relationship with another passenger, Reo Fortune, a charming young man from New Zealand on his way to study in England. He had a fellowship for graduate study at Cambridge University in which his focus was to be on dreams. A brilliant student and widely read, Fortune's interests in psychology and anthropology were soon to win him wide recognition.

Aboard the *Chitral*, Margaret and Reo had much time for discussing their shared interests, and in the process they also fell in love. It was therefore with very mixed emotions that Margaret met Luther at Marseilles, and their tour of France was cut short by the sudden appearance of Fortune at their hotel in Paris. The three then went their separate ways—Margaret to begin work at the American Museum of Natural History in New York, Luther to a job teaching sociology at the College of the City of New York (he was becoming disenchanted about a career in the ministry), and Reo to his studies at Cambridge University. Although Margaret and Luther briefly shared an apartment in New York, it soon became clear to both that their marriage was ending. The divorce, at Margaret's initiative, did not occur until 1928, and she and Reo were married shortly thereafter in New Zealand. They were then on their way to the Admiralty Islands, northeast of New Guinea, where they would both be doing field research.

Fortune had selected the site of Manus Island for their combined investigations, in which he was to focus especially on matters of religion and mythology and his new wife was to emphasize the study of young children. He was already familiar with the region from his recent field work on a nearby island (which later, in 1932, was published as *Sorcerers of Dobu*). On Manus, they selected the village of Peri as their primary location. This settlement had a population of only about 200, with houses built above water on stilts. Mead and Fortune had a similar home built for themselves to allow them to become a regular part of village life. Here, as in Samoa, Mead's primary kind of research was participant observation, though at Manus her emphasis was upon young children rather than adolescents.

Growing up in New Guinea (published in 1930) was title of the book in which Mead reported her observations on Manus. Here she describes early childhood as relatively free and pleasant. However, she says,

> Unaided by the rich hints for play which children of other societies take from the admired adult traditions, they have a dull, uninteresting child life, romping good humoredly until they are tired, then lying inert and breathless until rested sufficiently to romp again.

Ultimately it is the competitive and materialistic adult world that takes over after this relatively free early childhood.[5]

In the summer of 1929, Mead and Fortune completed their studies on Manus and returned to the United States. Mead soon learned how popular her *Coming of Age in Samoa* had proved to be, and she worked on her manuscript for *Growing up in New Guinea*. She and Fortune, who had a fellowship to study at Columbia University, uncomfortably settled into their humdrum life in a fourth floor walk-up apartment in the area near Margaret's work at the American Museum and Reo's work at Columbia.

The following year they combined grants for fieldwork among the Omaha tribe of Native Americans in Nebraska. It was not a very satisfying project for either of them (Mead later called it "a devastating experience"), and they began to lay plans for a return to fieldwork across the Pacific. This time, in the summer of 1931, their sights were set on the island of New Guinea itself, starting in a mountainous region near the northeast coast.[6]

Mead and Fortune were in New Guinea for almost two years, living there with three tribes. First they studied the Mountain Arapesh, a gentle and good-natured people, then the more aggressive Mundugumor, and finally they observed the unexpected patterns of the Tchambuli. Mead was to describe these three in her *Sex and Temperament in Three Primitive Societies* (published in 1935) as societies with very different views of basic human temperaments. Among the Arapesh both men and women emphasize the styles that we in the West tend to view as feminine; with the Mundugumor both sexes appear to show what to us are masculine temperaments, while the Tchambuli expected women to be the more materialistic and aggressive and the men to have more artistic interests—an apparent reversal of the sex roles most common in the West.[7]

From such differences observed in societies just about a hundred miles from each other, Mead concluded that the role of culture in shaping sex-typed behavior is almost unbelievably strong. As in her conclusions in *Coming of Age in Samoa*, she drew from her New Guinea observations important implications for American society. She emphasized that we should prepare for a greater diversity in what we expect of American men and women. As she concludes in *Sex and Temperament*:

> If we are to achieve a richer culture, rich in contrasting values, we must recognize the whole gamut of human potentialities, and so weave a less arbitrary social fabric, one in which each diverse human gift will find a fitting place.

She was to return later to the same theme when she published, in 1949, *Male and Female: A Study of the Sexes in a Changing World*. There she emphasized that "We can build a whole society only by using both the gifts special to each sex and those shared by both sexes—by using the gifts of the whole of humanity."[8]

The very personal world of Margaret Mead underwent an important change while she was still in New Guinea. She and Fortune joined other anthropologists in December 1932 for a rambunctious end-of-year party in a town far up the Sepik River, and it was there that they met Gregory Bateson. An English anthropologist then studying a coastal tribe, Bateson had many exciting discussions with Mead and Fortune, and Margaret seemed especially impressed with the ideas of this new friend. They then spent some months in study sites near each other, and Gregory and Margaret soon became very close friends. By the time they left New Guinea a clear change in her affections had occurred, although it was not until 1935 that she finally divorced Reo (and married Bateson the following year).

Margaret Mead planned to work with Bateson on the East Indies island of Bali, and the two of them were married in Singapore on their way to their new fieldwork. They were to focus especially on issues of mental illness in a different culture. Bateson, tall and erudite, had a strong background in psychological studies, and Mead increasingly was trying to apply psychoanalytic ideas to her work. Bali seemed a natural place to test their ideas about psychological abnormality in relation to cultural patterns.

The Balinese appeared to have features of both general apathy and psychological intensity. They seemed quite relaxed in much of their daily life, but ceremonial occasions brought out an intensity of dancing that could culminate in a deep trance. Here was a most interesting culture for both of them to study, and they were on Bali for two years. During this time they developed new research techniques which combined Margaret's skills at interviewing and observation with Gregory's imaginative use of the camera. This ultimately produced their *Balinese Character: A Photographic Analysis*, published in 1942.

After more than two years on Bali plus a side trip to New Guinea, Mead and Bateson were ready to return to the West. This was in 1939, and their lives were soon to be caught up in the events of World War II. This did not seem to be an appropriate time to continue their cooperative fieldwork. In addition, their lives were soon enriched by the arrival of a child, Mary Catherine Bateson, born December 8, 1939.

Although she was to do some further fieldwork after the war (most notably in a return to Manus in 1953), Mead's life became more centered in New York after the work on Bali. Still, however, she saw her fieldwork as the primary contribution she made to anthropology. "Anthropology is fieldwork," she was to emphasize in *Anthropologists and What They Do*, published in 1965. Later in her introduction to *Letters From the Field 1925-1975* (published in 1977) she continued to assert that "Field work has provided the living stuff out of which anthropology has developed as a science and which distinguishes this from all other sciences."[9]

In her later years Margaret Mead was to engage in many activities other than anthropological fieldwork—indeed, many activities beyond anthropology—but she always remained best known for her early observations of cultures in far-off lands. Part of this renown rested upon the graceful style of her writing. But this was supported by her skilled interviewing and detailed field notes. She provided, as another anthropologist said after her death, "a vividness unmatched and unrivaled in the professional anthropological literature."[10]

At, and Beyond, the Museum

Upon her return to New York from Samoa, Margaret Mead became an assistant curator of anthropology at the American Museum of Natural History. From then, in 1926, until her death she was closely associated with the museum. She was promoted to associate curator in 1942, and received the full status as curator of ethnology in 1964.

By choice Mead established herself high in one of the towers of the museum, where she would be little bothered by routine museum visitors. She did help organize a number of exhibits, but mostly she was left free to do the kind of work she wished. The museum also was generous in granting research leaves and assisted in obtaining funding for some of her projects. Once established there, the museum became a home base for her work for the rest of her life.

Mead worked hard and was quite demanding of those who worked with her. In her tower quarters she developed a steady flow of research assistants, nearly all young women. Mostly they were very pleased to work for the great Margaret Mead, but the pace was often hectic. She was involved in many activities besides museum affairs, and she found a way to handle most of these projects from her tower office.

During World War II, Mead and Bateson were active on the Committee on National Morale, designed to involve social scientists in the war effort. As a more specific contribution, she took leadership for a Committee on Food Habits of the National Research Council. In this project efforts were made to influence foods that Americans selected in the interests of good nutrition and the food needs of others. As the war was ending a central activity, run from her tower office, became the Institute for Intercultural Studies (or IIS). This organization was designed officially to:

> create a climate of opinion of the importance of the cultural approach, to facilitate informal relationships between students of national character, to prepare and distribute reprints for those interested in developing or applying the cultural approach to contemporary international problems, to develop new research and new research methods and to apply the cultural approach to problems of intercultural adjustment between and within nations.

This statement summarized well what Mead's primary interests were at that time.[11]

Increasingly Mead became involved in work on "national character" and what was becoming known as applied anthropology. In their new culture-and-personality studies Mead and her close friends Ruth Benedict and Geoffrey Gorer sought to summarize psychological characteristics of an entire society. Mead's most notable work of this kind was her 1942 book on American character, *And Keep Your Powder Dry*. Benedict's impressive study of Japanese culture, *The Chrysanthemum and the Sword*, came out in 1946, and Gorer contributed books on *The American People* (1948) and *English Character* (1955). These efforts of studying "culture at a distance," involving a minimum of direct fieldwork, were seen by many anthropologists as providing too broad and free generalizations about complex modern societies, and the interests of anthropologists in such broad culture-and-personality studies generally declined after the 1950s.

A much more favorable response was given to Mead's efforts to promote applied anthropology. Anthropological studies could be made of any number of settings within modern complex societies. Such studies could be useful as basic studies of human behavior, and they also often had implications for public policy.

Mead was busily engaged in such activities at the same time that she was raising a daughter. Her work was little affected by the addition of Mary Catherine to the household, and the child grew up with what was essentially an extended family of Mead's friends. Her marriage also often took second place to her work, and Gregory was away for increasing periods of time. In 1950, Gregory and Margaret were divorced, primarily at his initiative. Bateson would later reflect that

> I couldn't keep up and she couldn't stop. She was like a tugboat. She would sit down and write three thousand words by eleven o'clock in the morning and spend the rest of the day working at the museum.[12]

Columbia University was where Mead not only received her training as an anthropologist but also the primary institution where she sought to pass on her learning to others. She was a popular teacher there, serving many years as an adjunct professor. She chose, however, to keep her primary identification with the museum, twice turning down offers from Columbia for a tenured appointment as full professor in anthropology. The museum allowed her the flexibility to teach when, and as much as, she wanted, and she taught for brief periods at a number of different locations, not to mention the special lectures she gave at colleges and universities all over America. As one of her biographers commented, "Whatever else Margaret Mead was doing, and wherever she happened to be, she never stopped teaching."[13]

When she reached the normal retirement age, she was pleased that the museum allowed her to continue in her post without any significant change. The museum also allowed her freedom to return to some of the sites of her earlier fieldwork. The most significant of her return trips was to the island of Manus in 1953, the setting for her early report on *Growing Up in New Guinea*. She found a drastically changed society there, as earlier traditions made way for adaptations to the modern world. She reported her impressive findings about these changes in *New Lives for Old* (published in 1960).[14]

Mead kept up her frenetic schedule of meetings, speaking engagements, and writing for the rest of her life. She was easily America's best-known anthropologist, writing for her very wide audience with regular features in *Redbook* magazine and feeling quite free to speak her mind on any number of subjects as she traveled around the country. Her range of activities included lay services for the Episcopal Church, work for the World Foundation for Mental Health and UNESCO, and the presidency of the American Association for the Advancement of Science.

Even though suffering from an advancing case of pancreatic cancer, which she resisted admitting, Mead kept to an active schedule into the year of her death. In August of 1978 she kept her engagements to speak at a Chautauqua Institution meeting in northwestern New York and at the convention of the American Correctional Association in Portland, Oregon. But by then her failing health had become apparent. Her death came in a New York hospital on November 15, 1978.

The Limits of Discovery

When Louis Leakey discovered a hominid jawbone near Lake Victoria in 1931, he felt that he had found clear evidence that Africa had been the location of the emergence of humanity. However, as we have seen, the evidence then at hand did not impress many of the experts. Only with further discoveries and more adequate documentation of them did Louis and Mary Leakey convince the world of the African origins of mankind.

The Leakeys had to demonstrate the meaning of specific bits of bone and stone they found in the hills and gullies of Africa. The task of demonstrating the varieties of human culture was a bit more complicated for Margaret Mead. She could record her observations and collect her artifacts, but her main task was to demonstrate the meaning of a pattern of findings. This was more difficult than the discovery of specific facts. Nevertheless, Mead had great skill in convincing readers that the cultural patterns she described were real.

Might Margaret Mead have been sometimes too skillful in the way she wrote about her research? Could her literary skills sometimes have allowed for her conclusions to come too easily? That question was very seriously raised at the end of her career, and her very earliest fieldwork in Samoa (reported in her most popular book) became a subject of special controversy.

Five years after Mead's death saw the publication of a book by Derek Freeman, *Margaret Mead and Samoa: The Making and Unmaking of an Anthropological Myth,* In this book, published by Harvard University Press, Freeman took issue with Mead's description of Samoan culture. His own intensive studies of Samoa suggested that what she had described in her first book was a very one-sided picture. Life was not so peaceful on that island, and adolescence was not that free and easy. Had she been too eager to support the thesis of cultural relativity expounded by her mentor, Franz Boas? Had she tended to turn a blind eye to biological factors involved in Samoan adolescence?[15]

Although Margaret Mead was no longer alive to take part in the debate, her colleagues came to her defense. As with so many debates, the results were inconclusive. What Mead had found in 1925 and 1926 in a small village on a remote island may have been different from what Freeman many years later was to find elsewhere in Samoa. Her earliest work on Samoa may not have had the sophistication of her later fieldwork elsewhere. All of this may be true, but was not Freeman a bit too free in indulging in polemics?

The discovered facts of social science do not speak for themselves. They must be interpreted within the context in which they are found, and by a community of scientists with special knowledge in the areas involved. Mead would certainly agree with this general conclusion. That is, after all, what science is all about. The refinements about the meaning of discoveries must remain forever open. So also must it be the case with Margaret Mead's studies of cultural variation.

5

B.F. Skinner and the Principles of Operant Behavior

From the Hills of Susquehanna

Burrhus Frederic Skinner began life on March 20, 1904, in Susquehanna, Pennsylvania. He continued to live in the same house there in which he was born until the year he went to college. He grew up comfortably in a stable family, the son of a respected attorney and his equally respectable wife. Susquehanna was a small railroad town among the hills of northeastern Pennsylvania, so small that there were only eight students in Skinner's high school graduation class. But the area surrounding the town was a lovely place for boys to explore, and young Fred and his friends made the most of it.

Even while loving to wander around outdoors, the young boy also early acquired a passion for things to do inside, especially reading. The Skinner home had a good collection of books, supplementing those of the town library and school. He also developed a love for music, learning to play the piano, and, later, the saxophone.

One notable feature of Fred's early life was his desire to make and invent things. As he recalled years later in a brief autobiographical account:

> I was always building things. I built roller-skate scooters, steerable wagons, sleds, and rafts to be poled about on shallow ponds. I made seesaws, merry-go-rounds, and slides. I made slingshots, bows and arrows, blow guns and waterpistols from lengths of bamboo, and from a discarded water boiler a steam cannon with which I could shoot plugs of potato and carrot over the houses of our neighbors. I made tops, diabolos, model airplanes driven by twisted rubber bands, box kites, and tin propellers which could be sent high into the air with a spool-and-string spinner. I tried again and again to make a glider in which I myself might fly.[1]

School had an unusual appeal for the young Skinner. As he later said, "I *liked* school" and he recalled his habit of arriving early to be let in

before the other students arrived. "I was a constant problem for the jani-
tor...but he would shrug, open the door just enough to let me through,
and lock it after me." A special influence was a teacher named Mary
Graves. She had a great love for art and literature and showed a special personal interest in her talented student, who later said that "Miss
Graves was probably responsible for the fact that in college I majored in
English literature and afterwards embarked upon a career as a writer."[2]

In the fall of 1922, Skinner began his work at Hamilton College in
Clinton, New York. He entered college with a great desire to study and
learn. However, he soon found, as he wrote at the end of his first year,
that only a few students enjoyed studies or went to the library volun-
tarily, and that "he was almost alone in his pursuit of literature, and
that he was actually jeered at for spending time on a book when other
boys were supporting athletics." Although he made an adjustment to his
world of fellow students and accepted reduced scholarly aspirations, his
academic interests (especially for language study and music) survived.
But he also developed a cynical attitude and became adept at devising
practical jokes to make fun of college practices, some of which showed
in his work for the student newspaper. As he later recalled,

> Through the student publications we began to attack the faculty and various local
> sacred cows. I published a parody of the bumbling manner in which the professor of
> public speaking would review student performances at the end of a class. I wrote an
> editorial attacking Phi Beta Kappa. At commencement time I was in charge of Class
> Day exercises, which were held in the gymnasium, and with the help of another
> student... [we] covered the walls with bitter caricatures of the faculty.[3]

But there were positive experiences at Hamilton as well. He became
a tutor for a son of the dean, and he came to enjoy his relationships with
that family. He generally showed good work in his studies, eventually
achieving Phi Beta Kappa honors. He developed further his skill as a
writer. When a senior he sent some of his short stories to the poet Robert
Frost and received an encouraging response. Because of such recognition for his work, he finished college with the intention to become a
writer.

Skinner returned to live with his parents (now in Scranton, Pennsylvania, where his father had become general counsel for a coal company). He set up a work place in the attic and began to write. However,
no Great American Novel came forth. As he later commented,

> The results were disastrous. I frittered away my time. I read aimlessly, built model
> ships, played the piano, listened to the newly-invented radio, contributed to the hu-
> morous column of a local paper but wrote almost nothing else, and thought about
> seeing a psychiatrist.

Through his father's work came an opportunity for a very different kind of writing than Skinner first imagined. There was a need to make abstracts of court decisions affecting the coal industry. The young Skinner turned to this task (nominally working with his father but actually doing the work himself), and the result was a privately printed book, *A Digest of Decisions of the Anthracite Board of Conciliation.* After this book came an interlude of six months in New York, where Skinner entered into the bohemian life of Greenwich Village, and a leisurely summer trip through Europe. Then he was ready for graduate work at Harvard.[4]

Skinner later summarized what he learned during this period of his life: "I discovered the unhappy fact that I had nothing to say, and went on to graduate study in psychology, hoping to remedy that shortcoming."[5]

Brave New Psychologist

Skinner had taken no course in psychology at Hamilton College. In literature and science courses he found references to psychological subject matter, but this did not seem important at the time. Psychology became important only after he failed to find his niche as a writer.

His first enthusiasm for psychology came through reading books by Bertrand Russell and Ivan Pavlov. He read with interest what Russell wrote about psychology in magazine articles, then bought and read copies of recent books by Russell and John B. Watson. He saw in what behavioral psychologists were doing a model for his own future. Years later he would meet Russell and comment on his role in making him a behaviorist in psychology. "Good Heavens!" responded Lord Russell, "I had always supposed that those articles had demolished Behaviorism!"—but apparently not so far as the young Skinner was concerned.[6]

What especially confirmed Skinner's interest in psychology was a story in the *New York Times* where H. G. Wells was quoted with favorable comments about a Russian referred to as "Professor Pavloff." Skinner got a copy of Pavlov's latest work, *Conditioned Reflexes*, and found there an area of study he wished to make his own.

But where should he go to study psychology? After consulting some of his friends and former teachers, Skinner concluded that Harvard was the best place. Accordingly, he sent an application to enter the Harvard graduate program in psychology. Harvard accepted his application, and he was off to begin his studies there in the fall of 1928.

Later Skinner was to describe his adjustment to Harvard as rather severe:

> At Harvard I entered upon the first strict regimen of my life. I had done what was expected of me in high school and college but had seldom worked hard. Aware that I was far behind in a new field, I now set up a rigorous schedule and maintained it for almost two years. I would rise at six, study until breakfast, go to classes, laboratories, and libraries with no more than fifteen minutes unscheduled during the day, study until exactly nine o'clock at night and go to bed. I saw no movies or plays, seldom went to concerts, had scarcely any dates, and read nothing but psychology and physiology.

Still later he was to admit that this description was something of an exaggeration—more a "pose" than the full reality of his daily life—but it nevertheless describes the attitude Skinner took toward his studies at Harvard.[7]

Despite his limited background in psychology, Skinner's hard work and interest in the great variety of opportunities at Harvard soon bore fruit. He developed his own laboratory facilities and went to work studying the conditioning of squirrels from Harvard yard and different strains of laboratory rats. He worked initially in facilities assigned to physiology, though maintaining his graduate status in psychology. He claims that in his special projects courses: "I worked entirely without supervision. No one knew what I was doing until I handed in some flimsy report." Apparently the psychologists assumed that he was being directed by the physiologists, and they in turn "thought someone in psychology was keeping an eye on me." In reality, however, he reports that "I was doing exactly as I pleased."[8]

Skinner's progress toward the doctoral degree was unusually swift. His work, though considered uneven by his professors (who themselves represented a wide variety of interests), was recognized as of outstanding promise. He was encouraged to use one of his papers as the core for a dissertation. He did this, passed his examinations, and soon saw this paper ("The Concept of the Reflex in the Description of Behavior") published. In 1931 he was awarded the Ph.D.

Staying on at Harvard for several more years (the last two as a distinguished "Junior Fellow," a newly established way of recognizing unusual talent at Harvard), Skinner was free to pursue his own studies. The rats and pigeons in his laboratory were at the center of his attention. He was always looking for new ways to isolate particular behaviors and develop reliable measures for his observations.

Skinner adapted a simple recording machine so that it would make a continuous measurement of any selected item of behavior. This developed a "cumulative record," where the slope of the curve could be seen as an indication of changes in response strength. He also sought new ways of identifying particular behaviors. Occasionally he would apply mathematical analyses to his results, though this was never his major interest. What he most wanted to find was clear results that would show predictable changes in specific behaviors.

Skinner wrote often to his parents, and in one letter he conveyed something of his intellectual thrill about the discoveries he was making:

> I have demonstrated that the rate in which a rat eats food, over a period of two hours, is a square function of the time. In other words, what heretofore was supposed to be 'free' behavior on the part of the rat is now shown to be just as much subject to natural laws as, for example, the rate of his pulse.

One of his most promising ideas was to allow the animal to initiate the behavior to be measured. Pressing a bar, for example, might be the occasion for making a pellet of food available. The experimenter would need to provide no special stimulus but could simply record results initiated by the animal in a strictly contained setting. Thus was born what became known as the "Skinner box," which was soon widely used by many psychologists for research in animal behavior. For Skinner it represented not just a new experimental technique, but a way of looking at behavior independently of specific stimuli. The responses of the animal were controlled by the consequences of behavior, not by specifically controlling stimuli.[9]

Soon Skinner was distinguishing between two basically different types of conditioning. There was, first of all, the typical stimulus-response conditioning made famous by Ivan Pavlov and John B. Watson. Here the stimulus controlled the response, and the study of conditioning was a study of how different stimuli might be combined in producing responses. Skinner came to call this "Type S" conditioning. Quite different was what he called "Type R" conditioning. In this second type the response was controlled by its consequences. Behavior here was not so much in response to a specific stimulus but a cumulative result of what followed the response. This second type of conditioning provided a way of looking at the behavior of the organism as a whole that does not need to be tied to specific stimuli. Skinner viewed the study of this new model of behavior ("operant behavior," as he came to call it) as much more promising for progress in the discipline of psychology.

The key concept in operant psychology is "reinforcement"—viewed as anything that increases an organism's probability of making a response. Soon Skinner was documenting the effects of different frequencies of reinforcement upon behavior. He was then led to study how behavior was systematically related to other differences in the manner of providing reinforcement. Although this was a natural progression for his work, he has also recognized accidental elements in this development. As he later recalled, one Saturday he noticed that he did not have enough food pellets to last through the weekend. He did have enough if only one pellet was used each minute, so he simply programmed his apparatus to deliver one pellet per minute—so long as the rat pressed the bar at least once in that time. He found that the responses of his animals maintained themselves at a steady rate. This led him to wonder about how other patterns of reinforcement might affect behavior. Thus was born his concern for "schedules of reinforcement." Soon a wide variety of different patterns of reinforcement—with such variations in schedules as "fixed ratio" (in which reinforcement was based on the number of responses) and "fixed interval" (based on time measures) joining the original technique of "continual reinforcement" (reinforcement of each targeted response).

All of this research was to be described in scientific detail in Skinner's book, *The Behavior of Organisms*, published in 1938. Only a few hundred copies were published initially, but this book was soon recognized as one of the most important works in the field of psychology. Skinner not only gave here detailed descriptions of his own studies, but he also expressed his vision of psychology as a science of behavior. By focusing on measures of actual behavior and the conditions under which such behavior occurs it was possible to avoid attending to much of what other psychologists were studying. Instead of the study of *mind*, psychology could become the science of *behavior*.[10]

From Harvard, and Back

By the time his *Behavior of Organisms* was published, Skinner had gone to teach at the University of Minnesota. With his privileged years as a junior fellow at Harvard ending in 1936, he had to seek more normal employment. During the same year, his marriage to Yvonne Blue brought family responsibilities. Later the Skinner family was joined by two daughters, Julie and Debbie.

At Minnesota, Skinner continued his studies of operant behavior, which now also began to take a more applied emphasis. As World War II approached, he thought about how unmanned missiles might be guided by birds which could be systematically trained to steer them correctly.

This seemed to military reviewers to be expecting a lot of the pigeons Skinner was training, and his project never received government support. However, he continued to feel it might have worked.

During this period, Skinner gave increased emphasis to how rewarding successive approximations to desired behavior could yield impressive behavior changes. "Shaping" was the name he gave to this form of operant behavior. He has described one impressive example as follows:

> We put a pigeon in a large cardboard carton, on one wall of which was a food dispenser operated by a hand switch. We put a wooden ball the size of a Ping-Pong ball on the floor and undertook to teach the pigeon to knock it about the box. We began by reinforcing merely looking at the ball, then moving the head toward it, then making contact with it, and eventually knocking it to one side with a swiping motion. The pigeon was soon batting the ball about the box like a squash player. We had shaped a very complex topography of behavior through successive approximation in a matter of minutes.

Although Skinner, as well as other psychologists, had applied the same basic technique before, he remembered that particular time as one of "great illumination," and henceforth "shaping" would have a central role to play in both basic research and applications of operant conditioning.[11]

More and more Skinner and like-minded operant psychologists turned to technical applications of their ideas. One of the most publicized results was the development of an "air crib" in which a baby might be placed for most hours of the day and night in a scientifically controlled environment. The Skinners applied this idea to the early care of their second child. Many readers were horrified when they saw this mechanical baby-tending device seriously described on the pages of *Ladies' Home Journal*, but Skinner considered it a good idea and sought—but with little success—to move it into industrial production.

Even more ambitious projects for Skinner were the operant analysis of verbal behavior and the design for an entire society. He often taught courses in the psychology of literature and had a special interest in the way people talked. Over a period of many years (his first draft of a book was in 1941), he worked on the study of verbal behavior. Finally, in 1957 his *Verbal Behavior* was published. It was a controversial book among psycholinguists, many of whom felt that Skinner's behaviorism omitted the core of their field, but Skinner was at least credited with showing the great extent to which language behavior could be seen as a result of complex forms of conditioning.[12]

The design for an entire society based on principles of behavioral psychology was an even more ambitious project. Writing with unusual speed, Skinner took only seven weeks to write the first draft of *Walden Two*, his image of a behavioral utopia. Initially he had difficulty in finding a publisher for this exercise in psychological fiction, but eventually the book appeared in 1948 and soon became a best seller. He has described the book as "pretty obviously a venture in self-therapy, in which I was struggling to reconcile two aspects of my own behavior" shown by the chief characters. In general, the society of *Walden Two* illustrates what might be the result if positive reinforcement would be applied systematically to human society.[13]

In the fall of 1945, the Skinners moved to Bloomington, Indiana, where he became chair of the Indiana University psychology department. Two years later, Skinner was honored with the invitation to return to Harvard to deliver the William James Lectures (he chose verbal behavior as a special focus for his presentations), and while there he was offered a permanent position as a psychology professor. He accepted the offer, and lived the rest of his life at, or near, Harvard University.

An early project in Skinner's new career at Harvard was an undergraduate class he proposed which would focus on human behavior. Naturally his emphasis was on how what we know about behavioral psychology might be applied more widely to humans. Part of this he had previously set out in fictional form in *Walden Two*, but now he needed to give more systematic treatment to his ideas. These lectures led to his book, *Science and Human Behavior,* establishing him as a serious advocate of applying a behaviorist approach to the full range of human behaviors.[14]

Harvard also was the setting of renewed basic experimental research. With an unusually able group of graduate students, Skinner sought to refine his basic scientific findings. They rather ambitiously called their work, done primarily with pigeons, "the experimental analysis of behavior." Basically this research sought to pin down the detailed way that different contingencies of reinforcement lead to changes in behavior. He later called this period of experimental work "the high point of my research history."[15]

Soon the group led by Skinner was active in research centers all over America, and "the experimental analysis of behavior" became a phrase describing their studies of operant behavior. In many of these a distinctly applied emphasis was present, and soon "behavior modification" became a well-known phrase in fields as different as clinical psychology, penology, and education. Skinner himself took a leading role in educational applications, including efforts for programmed instruction and the development of teaching machines.

B.F. Skinner's contributions to social science would have been well established if he had written nothing beyond *The Behavior of Organisms*. That he continued in his systematic research efforts for many more years only consolidated his status as a leading social scientist. The applications he and his associates made of operant principles for the control of behavior gave him even wider recognition. And all his work was tied together in the philosophic stance he assumed as a behaviorist. During the final decades of his career he became one of the best known scholars of the twentieth century, and the key element in his popularity—and notoriety—was his espousal of the philosophy of behaviorism.

Discovery and Theory

Discoveries in social science are facilitated by the theoretical orientations of the discoverers. For example, Louis Leakey's assumptions about the early evolution of humans in Africa—developed before there was any conclusive evidence to support it—was a key factor in the way the Leakeys conducted their explorations and made their discoveries. Margaret Mead, to take another example, would never have identified the dramatic cultural patterns she did in and around Samoa, New Guinea, and Bali if she had not started with the view of her mentor Franz Boas that culture was a highly variable factor in human behavior. B.F. Skinner also provides an example of the influence of his theoretical background upon the process of discovery. His most notable discoveries all came out of his philosophy of behaviorism.[16]

Skinner's philosophy was scientific in a radically empirical way. His primary purpose as a scientist was to discover regular relationships between classes of observable events. From such relationships causal inferences could be made. That, in his view, is the central nature of science.

Skinner may also be described as a proponent of "operationism," which he defined as

> ...the practice of talking about (1) one's observations, (2) the manipulative and calculational procedures involved in making them, (3) the logical and mathematical steps which intervene between earlier and later statements, and (4) nothing else.

The major virtue Skinner saw in operationism lies in the fourth point: it helps us avoid excess baggage in getting on with the business of objective science.[17]

Although widely known as a "learning theorist," Skinner was not particularly interested in "theory" as most commonly understood by others. One of his most noted theoretical articles was titled "Are Theories of Learning Necessary?" His own answer to this question seems to be "No." That is, most of what goes under the rubric of learning theory is unnecessary. The phenomena of learning, Skinner believed, can best be studied in terms of simply analyzing functional relations of responses and previous conditions. This does not require a theory about what goes on within the organism. Of course, there is room for "theory" in the sense of summary statements of patterns of observed relationships, but there is no need for any appeal to mental processes in order to explain behavior. Behavior, he felt, should always to be explained by identifying the objective stimulus conditions in which it occurs (including the past history of reinforcement of the organism).[18]

Skinner did not hesitate to assert that the control of human beings was a central purpose in his philosophy of behaviorism. This is made clear in *Beyond Freedom and Dignity,* published in 1971. In this work Skinner begins with the basic assumption that to solve human problems we need to apply some kind of technology; for most human problems this needs to be a technology of behavior. However, he believes that such a technology can be effective only if joined with a philosophy that redefines into more naturalistic terms the human needs identified with such concepts as "freedom" and "dignity."[19]

A behavioral technology is not a dream, Skinner insists. It is already in the process of development. Its key lies in the management of contingencies of reinforcement. This will allow us a better capability to control behavior toward those ends we see as generally desirable. Yes, control is needed, and there is no reason to balk at using this concept. Every time we systematically act upon the environment in order to affect others we exert control. But we do need to be clearer about the *objectives* of control and to be more effective in selecting the *means* of control.

Skinner continued to promote his philosophy of behaviorism to the end of his days. Although he was universally recognized for his scientific achievements, Skinner found his philosophical stance a center of controversy—both among his fellow psychologists and with the general public. But he seemed to thrive on that controversy. He resisted what he admitted was the increasing use of cognitive models in psychology and continued to insist that psychology should be simply seen as the science of behavior. He expressed himself rather clearly in opposition to psychology as a study of "mind," asserting in one of the last things he wrote, "So far as I'm concerned, cognitive science is the creationism of psychology."[20]

In 1989, Skinner was diagnosed with leukemia. Even as the illness progressed, he maintained his daily schedule as much as possible. He completed his last article on August 18, 1990. He died later that same day.

Part 3

Theorists

6

John Dewey and the Social Logic of Inquiry

Becoming a Philosopher

No precocious intellect appeared in the boyhood of John Dewey. He did well in school, but his marks there were not outstanding. He went on to college at the University of Vermont largely because it was located in his home town of Burlington. It was only during his senior year there that his enthusiasm for academic studies became compelling, and the subject that especially caught his interest then was philosophy.[1]

John Dewey was known to his neighbors as a good boy. His mother was a primary influence in this, constantly reminding him of the moral demands of Christianity. His father, a storekeeper and solid citizen, made less of a fuss about religion, but the Deweys were faithful members of the local Congregational church. They were a middle-class family, well recognized among the leading circles of what was then a town of only about 11,000 in population.

Set along the shores of Lake Champlain, Burlington gave many opportunities for a lad to wander about and enjoy nature, a recreational activity that continued throughout Dewey's life. He also had ample opportunities for books. There were many good books in his home, and he early learned to make use of the public library. Although he did well in school and had a nearly perfect record for deportment, he did not find school a particularly exciting place. There was, a leader of the school system even then acknowledged, "too much learning and teaching parrotwise." This pattern of education was what Dewey later sought to change, but at the time no one would have dreamed that this shy young man was to lead a revolution in American education.[2]

It was during his last two years of college that John Dewey began to show an outstanding intellect, and it was in philosophy courses that Dewey's mind really caught fire. He had two able professors in this field. One was Matthew Buckman (who was also the president of the university) for political and social philosophy. Another was H.A.P. Torrey, who taught mental and moral philosophy. Dewey absorbed all that he could from these men, and he showed the highest quality of academic work that either had ever seen. Dewey had decided to try to become a philosopher himself.

But how does one make a living as a philosopher? College teaching was one possibility, but at that time most philosophy professors in American colleges had theological backgrounds. Dewey couldn't see himself as that kind of teacher. He continued to affirm his religious background, teaching a Sunday school class while a college student, but he had no religious calling when it came to philosophy. He sought a truth that would come from human reason rather than from religious inspiration.

So Dewey graduated from college without clear occupational plans. He had the educational preparation for high school teaching, and that would be what he would do for three years. But even during his years as a schoolteacher, he could not suppress his philosophic ambitions. He continued to take informal instruction from Professor Torrey, who encouraged him to go further in his studies. He also contributed to a *Journal of Speculative Philosophy*. His first effort there was titled "The Metaphysical Assumptions of Materialism." In this article he suggested that the implicit assumptions of a materialistic philosophy led to a dualism of mind and matter, which would allow for traditional views of moral and religious values. The editor not only accepted this article for publication (apparently it agreed with his own views) but he also gave personal encouragement for Dewey to continue his philosophical studies.

The Johns Hopkins University in Baltimore was then a new school that gave special emphasis to graduate education. It had quickly established a fine reputation for philosophy, and Dewey decided to study there. But when he applied for a special scholarship he was not successful, and another application for a smaller award was also turned down. Dewey, however, would not accept defeat, once he had decided what he wanted to do. He borrowed $500 from a relative and was off to Baltimore.

Dewey found at Johns Hopkins knowledgeable professors and a strong climate for student research. His interest soon turned to German works in philosophy and psychology. Kant and Hegel were generally recognized as the most powerful figures of modern philosophy, and Dewey gave special attention to these German idealists. Immanuel Kant had emphasized that inherent in the human mind were certain capacities for reason and that knowledge of the empirical world was filtered through innately given categories of thought. G.W.F. Hegel followed in Kant's tradition but gave a stronger emphasis to the role of spiritual qualities in human understanding. Basic reality, according to Hegel, lies in the ideas and ideals which empower all human activities. Above it all was the idea of the absolute—the universal mind which was the foundation of all reality.

In Hegel's philosophy Dewey found an answer to the troubling duality of mind and matter. One could be very hard-headed in studies of the empirical world and still retain the faith that there was some over-arching reality which gave purpose to it all. This over-arching reality was fundamentally a matter of spirit rather than anything material. God (or his philosophical equivalent) could still be in his heaven, with the world unfolding according to divine purposes.

George Sylvester Morris, a prominent Hegelian, had a special influence on Dewey. Morris, though based at the University of Michigan, came to Johns Hopkins each year to lecture on the history of philosophy. When Dewey finished his graduate work at Johns Hopkins (with a dissertation on "The Psychology of Kant") he was thrilled when Morris offered him a teaching position at Michigan. So it was that this promising young philosopher went to Ann Arbor, Michigan, in 1884 to begin his career as a college teacher. He helped his chief mentor to develop at Michigan a leading center for idealistic philosophy. Dewey found this philosophy quite compatible with his Christian convictions, and he soon became prominent in activities of the Students' Christian Association and was an active member of Ann Arbor's First Congregational Church.

Although Dewey's love affair with Hegelian philosophy continued, another love also became manifest in his early years at Ann Arbor. This concerned an energetic and very bright philosophy student named Alice Chapman. John and Alice first met as residents of the same Ann Arbor boarding house, but her interest in philosophy (she was a charter member of the Philosophical Society and a student in several of Dewey's classes) brought them together in other contexts. As their relationship became more personal, they began to talk about marriage, though this did not occur until 1886.

In 1888, Dewey accepted an appointment to head the philosophy program at the University of Minnesota, but this lasted only one year. The sudden death of Professor Morris led to an invitation for Dewey to return to the University of Michigan to head its philosophy department. He remained at Michigan until an unusual opportunity at the University of Chicago came in 1894.

Psychology, then still usually considered a part of philosophy, was the focus of much of Dewey's work at Michigan. This led to his first book, *Psychology*, published in 1887. This book became widely used as a textbook for psychology courses, and it was generally agreed that Dewey did a fine job of covering the latest experimental studies, largely coming out of German laboratories. What received less universal approval was the way these concrete studies were interpreted to support Hegelian ideas.

Dewey was not yet ready to give up his Hegelian philosophy. Only in 1900 was there evidence in his writings that a break had been made. However, gradually it became less important for him to point to ultimate abstractions about mental life when he discussed the facts of psychology or the realities of human moral choices. His daughter later suggested that Dewey's wife may have been an important part of this influence, for "things which had previously been matters of theory acquired through his contact with her a vital and direct human significance."[3]

Dewey's budding interest in education, expressed in activities for the Michigan Schoolmasters' Club, was another factor which appeared to reduce his need for a metaphysical idealism. Another key influence was William James, the Harvard psychologist and philosopher. Dewey later said that James' *Principles of Psychology*, published in 1890, had "worked its way more and more into all my ideas and acted as a ferment to transform old beliefs." In any event, when he went to the University of Chicago in 1894, Dewey's basic philosophy had begun moving toward American pragmatism and away from German idealism.[4]

At Chicago

Although still only thirty-four years of age when he was offered a position at the University of Chicago, John Dewey was already established as a leader in both psychology and philosophy. This was confirmed by the nature of his offer—he was invited to head a department of philosophy which was to include programs in both psychology and pedagogy. William Rainey Harper, the president of this relatively new but well-endowed university, sought an outstanding faculty to develop an early reputation for advanced studies.

Soon after arriving at Chicago, Dewey proposed that pedagogy be recognized as a separate department. This would allow it to be more effective in training specialists in education and to carry on research concerning educational procedures. A laboratory school for the teaching of elementary students was to become an integral part of the new department. President Harper readily agreed with these proposals, and the Department of Pedagogy and a University Elementary School were soon established. Dewey was to direct both of these programs, while still continuing to head the Department of Philosophy.

Dewey turned enthusiastically to make his laboratory school a showcase for new methods of education. No longer were children to be treated as subjects for rote learning, but they were to be involved actively in what was learned. This focus on the child as an active learner was a primary theme of the school, and the research coming out of its experimental programs seemed supportive of this new approach.

More and more Dewey turned his talents to writing about education. He emphasized that children are from the beginning active learners and that teachers should use these natural tendencies in whatever programs they developed for them. The child, not abstract subject matter, must be at the heart of the curriculum, and children should be encouraged to explore what they may achieve for themselves. Further, their explorations should not sharply separate intellectual pursuits from motor skills. The more education could relate to the whole life of the child, the more successful should be its results.

Furthermore, minds are not just products of individual development, but they are formed in a social context. Schools must therefore provide for group activities to promote positive social development. By exploring their interests together with others, children naturally prepare themselves for the roles they must play in their later adult communities. As Dewey expressed this,

> The only way to prepare for social life is to engage in social life. To form habits of social usefulness and serviceableness apart from any direct social need and motive, and apart from any existing social situation, is, to the letter, teaching the child to swim by going through motions outside of the water.[5]

Two books expressing Dewey's philosophy of education were *The School and Society*, published in 1899, and *The Child and the Curriculum*, which appeared in 1902. Schools should be places where self development and social development go hand in hand, according to Dewey. All the means for this should be found in the school. "Learning?—certainly this," he said, in a summary of the purposes of education, "but living primarily, and learning through and in relation to this living."[6]

Writings such as these made Dewey a leader of what became known as "progressive education." His emphasis on "learning by doing" was to reverberate among professional educators for many decades to come. Such views remained in many educational circles controversial, but more and more leaders in the field of education came to subscribe to this new movement.

Dewey continued to write throughout his life on education, and he is probably most widely known as a philosopher of education. One of his most influential works, *Democracy and Education*, was to appear in 1916. He there attempted to spell out the kind of education which was needed for modern democratic society. Later in his life he was to criticize some of the things done in the name of "progressive education." For example, he once complained that "in some progressive schools the fear of adult imposition has become a veritable phobia." Dewey's most mature statement of his educational philosophy was to appear in *Experience and Education*, published in 1938. Here he emphasized that "a philosophy of education must be based on a philosophy of experience" and proceeded to stress the importance in human experience of continuity in personal growth and the interactive nature of persons with their environments.[7]

During his years at the University of Chicago, Dewey's attention to matters of educational theory and practice led him to question some of his more general philosophical assumptions. In his graduate seminars he found himself trying to treat Hegel in terms of revised principles and new terms. Then, as he later expressed it, "I came to realize that what the principles actually stood for could be better understood and stated when completely emancipated from Hegelian garb."[8]

By 1903 when Dewey and his associates published *Studies of Logical Theory*, the transition to a new framework had been completed. This new framework saw ideas as growing out of a functional relationship of persons and their environments. In psychology this general framework was becoming known as the school of "functionalism." In philosophy the term "pragmatism" became increasingly applied to such views. Truth was not some abstraction about ultimate reality but rather an awareness that arose out of the interactions of persons with their environment. What is true is what "works," that is, what meets the tests of one's own experience. What is right is also a matter of what works within the context of concrete moral choices, for there is no ultimate or final standard of right and wrong. There may be important moral principles, found to be useful in regulating one's life in a community, but these are not somehow written in the stars.

William James was specifically mentioned as a source for the ideas of *Studies of Logical Theory*, and he in turn responded warmly to Dewey and enthusiastically promoted this work among other scholars. "It is splendid stuff," James wrote to a friend, "and Dewey is a hero."

Although not always emphasizing the same themes (James gave more attention to consciousness in his psychology than was found in Dewey's more behaviorist orientation), James and Dewey remained in friendly contact until James' death in 1910, and both became recognized as leaders of the philosophy of pragmatism.[9]

Dewey's ideas about social reform were furthered during his years at Chicago. Although his writings (apart from those in the field of education) did not yet reflect this in a major way, he was active in a number of community endeavors. For example, he was a close friend of Jane Addams, a pioneer of the settlement house movement and a proponent of social reform more generally. Dewey was on the first Board of Trustees for Addams' Hull House and an active participant in its programs.

Because it was in the field of education that Dewey made his greatest impact while at Chicago, it is ironic that the success of his laboratory school led to his resignation there. A new unit for elementary teacher training with slightly different emphases from those of Dewey's laboratory school had been brought into the university, and there were now plans for the two schools to be merged. While Dewey was to direct this new combined program, there was a problem about the role of his wife. Alice Dewey had become the principal of her husband's laboratory school, and the Deweys assumed that her leadership would continue under the new arrangements. There was some objection raised about this, and President Harper felt he had reached a compromise with an appointment for Mrs. Dewey limited to one year. This, however, had not been clearly understood by the Deweys, and John felt that they had not been treated in good faith by their president. Rather than continue under an ambiguous set of relationships, Dewey chose to resign from the university.

At Columbia—and Beyond

Dewey had no immediate prospects of a new position when he resigned from the University of Chicago. Although expecting that a new teaching opportunity might soon appear, he set out with his family (he greatly enjoyed his family, and John and Alice then had five children) on a European vacation. While the Deweys were in Europe, special efforts were made at Columbia University to be able to create a position for Dewey there. Early in 1905 he became a member of Columbia's philosophy department, with an additional appointment to the faculty of Columbia's Teachers College. New York City then became Dewey's permanent home, and his relationship with Columbia was to continue for the rest of his career.

At Columbia, Dewey no longer had the kind of administrative duties which had been so much of his work at Chicago. He was freer to teach and write in accordance with his own interests. He continued as a leader in the philosophy of education. Books such as *How We Think* (in 1910) and *Democracy in Education* (1916) provide notable examples of this work. But he also made important contributions across the full range of philosophical topics, including such general works as *Reconstruction in Philosophy* (in 1920), as well as more focused contributions in fields such as ethics and logic. He continued work in psychology, which had been the subject of his first book, though now he gave special emphasis to social psychology. His most important publication in this field was *Human Nature and Conduct* (1922), in which he emphasized the role of the social group in shaping an individual's habits and impulses and sought to describe the emergence of intelligence as part of this social interplay.[10]

In addition to his scholarly endeavors, Dewey took on an increasingly prominent role as a general critic of national and international affairs and as a social activist. He felt free to take public stands on political issues of his times—such as initially opposing American entry into World War I but later supporting the war effort, or such as defending general rights for free speech and specific rights of labor to organize. His concept of democracy included what he called "industrial democracy," typically seen as realized through labor and professional organizations. He helped organize the American Association of University Professors (AAUP) and served as its first president. He assisted in founding New York's New School for Social Research, as well as the American Civil Liberties Union (ACLU). His articles on current affairs appeared frequently on the pages of the *New Republic* magazine. Sharing in the debate on public issues was for him a vital part of democracy.

Not only in America was Dewey's influence strongly felt, but his visits to Japan, China, and Turkey left a strong imprint of his ideas in those countries. He was recognized as a leading figure in the philosophy of education (and to a lesser extent, for philosophy in general) throughout the world.

Dewey's Theory of Knowledge

Although Dewey's influence was felt throughout the full range of philosophy, perhaps his most important contribution to the social sciences was in his theory of knowledge. This central philosophical subject, usually referred to as epistemology, was at the heart of his philosophy, and during the later part of his career he gave special attention to its central issues.

In the history of philosophy, there have been two major positions about the foundations of human knowledge. One is the "realist" tradition, and the other is often called an "idealist" point of view.

In the realist tradition, we start with a real world of physical nature, along with the human extensions of that nature. Knowledge consists of being able to reflect in ourselves that external reality. Our knowledge attains "truth" when we can demonstrate a close correspondence between our ideas and the external world outside our minds.

In the idealist tradition, knowledge is seen as ultimately a product of the human mind. It is always the mind that knows, using materials that are either inevitable features of the way our minds are constructed or ideas shaped by past experience. Our knowledge attains "truth" when we feel satisfied that contradictions among our ideas are eliminated.

Dewey started his philosophical career by trying to combine these two basic positions. As a supporter of modern science, he was naturally drawn to a realist position. However, his religious faith drew him toward an idealist viewpoint. For a time his solution was a compromise. In practical matters, including those regarding the education of human beings, he saw truth as whatever showed a correspondence to empirical observation. However, over all human knowing was the fundamental Hegelian "idea" or "spirit" that gradually unfolded with the growth of the collective mind. Human knowledge was seen as ultimately rooted in this sense of an absolute and over-arching mental structure of the essential nature of all things.

As he continued to develop his philosophy, Dewey gradually found his Hegelian idealism less needed. He found the sense that any truths could be located ultimately in the "mind" to fly in the face of what he was discovering about human education. But neither did a simple realist position work—for the mind is not just a passive product of experience. Gradually he came to view human knowledge as a product of the interaction between the developing person and the surrounding environment. With this as a starting point, he could build a theory of knowledge that drew on both realist and idealist traditions—but which fit simply into neither.

The basic position of Dewey, along with similar views of William James and others, came to be known as the "pragmatic" view of truth and knowledge. We know things to be true because their sense of truth "works" for us—that is, because the consequences of such beliefs seem to be supported by our later experience. This is basically the kind of truth seen in modern science—ideas are not true in and of themselves but are made true by their supporting evidence.

Dewey's form of pragmatism placed a great emphasis on the way people solve problems in their everyday lives. Their "knowing," he emphasized, develops as a part of this problem solving. Because of this emphasis, his philosophy is often referred to as "instrumentalism."

As Dewey saw it, we only think when faced with some kind of a problem or difficulty. We develop thought to help us solve our problems through a process of inquiry. This process has several typical stages. First, there is the felt difficulty or problem. Next there will be observation of whatever there is around us which might help us define more precisely the nature of the problem. Then will come an idea—an informal hypothesis or perhaps just a vague suggestion—about how the problem may be solved. A rational elaboration then follows as we "think" about the implications of such an idea. Finally, we come to some kind of action aimed at testing whether our idea of a solution is supported or not. If the idea is supported by the ensuing action, it will be considered to be "true."

Truth, in this view, always resides in our experience. Ideas come to be known as facts when supported by appropriate confirming experience. It is through action that their truth emerges, and not through some abstract logical process. When consequences of our actions fit what we anticipated, we see matters "truly," confirming as "facts" what had been present before as suggestions or hypotheses.

The process of developing knowledge, in Dewey's view, always resides in the particulars of experience. Things are not true in and of themselves, but only as our experience shows them to be true. This is as applicable to our everyday lives as to more formal tests of scientific hypotheses. We as individuals continually test out our private worlds to discover what is true for us.

We should also note that for Dewey there was always a collective dimension of our search for truth. We live our lives in communities of people, and our experience is not that of individuals separated from our social environments. The idea of an individual mind is to some degree always a fiction, for the person emerges as a self-conscious entity only through sharing in the world of others. There is thus always a social base for the experiences that confirm what we come to "know" as our truths. This applies not only to the way we act in everyday lives, but to the world of science in general. Scientific truth is what is generally determined by the community of scientists involved in a particular area of study. Here again is a close continuity between the worlds of science and those of our everyday experience.

Dewey's general philosophical ideas were most fully expressed in his book, *Experience and Nature*, first published in 1925. Here he outlined the principal elements of his metaphysics and epistemology. His viewpoint, which he now referred to as "empirical naturalism," sought to identify human experience as an extension of the natural world, and made the further elaboration of that world of nature dependent on our reasoned experience. As he expressed this view in the preface to his second (1929) and third (1958) editions of this work, "Experience is not a veil that shuts man off from nature; it is a means of penetrating continually further into the heart of nature." Although there is a sense in which nature always extends beyond our experience of it, what we can know about it is always contained in what we can in some way experience.[11]

A further general statement of Dewey's theory of knowledge came in 1938 with the publication of *Logic: The Theory of Inquiry*. This was a more sophisticated version of ideas he had presented much earlier (in works such as *How We Think*), along with a serious attempt to respond to the criticisms other philosophers had been making of his pragmatic viewpoints. He discusses the subject of logic as a part of "the matrix of inquiry" by which intellectual problems are addressed. In this context propositions are not so much either "true" or "false," but rather useful or not useful for clarifying the subject of inquiry. In fact, he preferred not to use the language of "truth," but rather terms such as "warranted conclusions" and "justified assertions." The general purpose behind such a preference was to help in "bringing logical theory into accord with scientific practice."[12]

The Activist Philosopher

When Dewey retired from Columbia in 1930, the university recognized him with the special title of Professor Emeritus of Philosophy in Residence and with the continuation of full pay. He continued his professional activity under such an arrangement until 1939, when he formally completed his retirement. Even then, he continued to write articles and turn out new editions of several of his books.

Such works as his *Logic*, in 1938, showed that retirement had little influence upon Dewey's main work as a scholar. As late as 1951 he was considering a new edition of *Experience and Nature*, for which he now planned to change the title to *Nature and Culture*. He continued to be active in public affairs until the year of his death.

John Dewey died on June 4, 1952, during a brief bout of pneumonia. He was then ninety-two years of age, with his lifespan (from his birth on October 20, 1859) extending from before the American Civil War to the Korean War. These were years of revolutionary changes in American society, changes that Dewey was constantly assimilating into his own thinking. These were also years of revolutionary changes in philosophy, changes in which Dewey himself played a leading role.

Of course, John Dewey did not lay to rest rival philosophical positions. Still continuing are the search for finding fundamental reality in an external physical world and the effort to establish abstract principles of truth within the human mind. But what Dewey has provided is a fresh philosophic position compatible with the methods of modern science. Even more pertinent do his theories appear for the development of social science. The relativity of knowledge to the process of knowing seems especially critical among the social sciences. Dewey sought to lay bare the social context of inquiry within which he felt that the social sciences must function.

7

Talcott Parsons and the Synthesis
of Social Theory

Academic Roots

The Reverend and Mrs. Edward Smith Parsons had five children, with the youngest, Talcott, born on December 13, 1902, in Colorado Springs, Colorado. The father, an ordained Congregational minister, had left his native New England to serve as a home missionary in Colorado, then became a teacher at Colorado College, the school his denomination had there established.[1]

Edward Parsons was a liberal Protestant of the "social gospel" movement. He optimistically considered how Christian ideals could reshape our world into a more cooperative society, and expressed his views in journal articles and a book, *The Social Message of Jesus*. He served at Colorado College as head professor of English from 1892 until 1917. During part of this time he also served as college dean and the school's vice president.

A campus controversy—apparently concerning improper relations of the president with female members of the staff—led to a split between Edward Parsons as vice president and the college president. In 1917, Parsons was dismissed from the school by its board of trustees, an action that led to an investigation by the American Association of University Professors. The AAUP's committee report later condemned the arbitrary nature of the firing and fully vindicated the actions of Parsons. By then, however, the Parsons family had moved to New York, where Talcott spent his last two years of high school in the Horace Mann School for Boys. In 1919 his father became president of Marietta College in Ohio, a position in which he continued until his retirement in 1936.

Talcott Parsons began studies at Amherst College (the school earlier attended by his father and two older brothers) in 1920. The school had become an important center of liberal education under the leadership of its president Alexander Meiklejohn. The reforms he had pioneered at Amherst included a change in the curriculum away from an elective system to a more comprehensive set of requirements. They also included the promotion of free inquiry and the examination of possible reforms in American society. Such changes were upsetting many Amherst alumni even while hailed elsewhere as an outstanding example of college reform. As a result of the controversy over his educational changes, Meiklejohn was forced to resign in 1923. Among the well considered defenses of Meiklejohn published at that time was an article in the *New Student* that Talcott Parsons wrote together with another Amherst student. This was to be the young Parsons' first published article.

When he entered Amherst, Talcott Parsons was expecting to become a doctor. His early studies there emphasized biology, which he chose as his major field (with philosophy as a second major area), but he also became attracted to the social sciences. He had an especially good introduction to institutional economics, and he read broadly through the social science literature. He graduated *magna cum laude* in 1924.

After graduation from college Parsons was offered support from a relative to study abroad for a year. He selected the London School of Economics, drawn by several of its faculty members who were well known as Social Democrats. Parsons by then had become a critic of capitalism and its culture, and he sought to learn more about socialist alternatives from such teachers as Harold Laski and Richard H. Tawney. This he did in London during 1924 and 1925; but even more was he there inspired by studying with several others on the faculty, such as the sociologists L.T. Hobhouse and Morris Ginsberg and the anthropologist Bronislaw Malinowski. In his classes with these men he received his first systematic introduction to sociology and a spur to the functional analysis of social systems.

In London, Talcott Parsons also met another American student named Helen Walker, who later, in 1927, became his wife. Talcott and Helen Parsons became the parents of three children, all born after their move to Cambridge, Massachusetts. Both were long associated with Harvard University, including Helen's work there with the Russian Research Center.

As his year in London was drawing to an end, an opportunity came for Parsons to continue his studies abroad. This was in the form of a fellowship from a German-American exchange program which would allow him to study in Germany. One of his teachers at Amherst, who was also on the selection committee of the exchange program, encouraged Parsons to apply. His application was soon accepted, and he was assigned to study at the University of Heidelberg. After a summer of intensive study of the German language, he was on his way to Heidelberg for the 1925-26 academic year.

The Discovery of Weber

His study at Heidelberg was to become one of the most pronounced influences upon the thinking of Talcott Parsons. As he was later to summarize his experience there:

> At Heidelberg I came into contact with what most would regard as the very best of German culture in the early part of the century, building on the great traditions of the German universities of the nineteenth century.... The dangers which eventuated in the Nazi movement were simply not evident at the time.[2]

It was in this pleasant intellectual atmosphere that Talcott Parsons became acquainted with Max Weber. He did not remember hearing of the work of Weber before going to Germany, and of course he never personally met Weber (who had died in 1920). But Max Weber continued as a giant in German social science, and Parsons soon found himself immersed in studying the works of Weber.

Several characteristics of Weber's work were to have an especially strong influence on Parsons. One was the breadth of Weber's contribution. Was Weber a historian, a sociologist, an economist, a political scientist, or what? He seemed to be all of these at the same time. He wrote careful historical analyses, but usually focused on the economic, political or religious forms of human society. He sought to understand the forms and sources of change in key social institutions in particular historical periods. A classic example was *The Protestant Ethic and the Spirit of Capitalism*. Here Weber sought to show how economic and religious institutions became intertwined in a particular period of Western history to produce the main outlines of modern capitalism. This book, incidentally, was first translated into English by Talcott Parsons.

Also characterizing Weber's work was his view of science as a vocation. It was important for Weber that the role of a social scientist be clearly set off from that of the citizen. The calling of science is the pursuit of truth, not social influence, and only with a "value-free" approach to the subject matter under investigation can scientific status be claimed. This does not mean that the social scientist as a person cannot promote the values desired for society—for example, Weber himself was quite active in German politics, energetically supporting liberal democratic causes—but he felt that such political efforts need to be clearly separated from the value neutral role of the social scientist.

Another feature of Weber's approach was the assumption that the fundamental stuff of human society has an inherently subjective nature. To understand developments in society we need to have a sense of how they are understood by the persons most directly involved. Therefore Weber emphasized what he called a "verstehen" approach. This required the scientific observer to go beyond the observation of behavior to study the meanings that individuals and groups expressed in their behavior. Weber saw no contradiction between this and his basic value neutrality. Only, he felt, by a disciplined control of our own values as social scientists can we clearly focus on the meanings and values of those that we study.

Finally, Weber's work was characterized by what has come to be known as the use of "ideal types" for theory building. There must be a simplification imposed in order to comprehend the complexities of social life, and Weber believed that a careful construction of concepts was essential. Using whatever is being studied to create purified images of that reality allows us to make important theoretical comparisons and, ultimately, tease out causal inferences.

Add to such general features of Weber's work the great variety of subjects he pursued (fundamentals of social stratification, authority structures, the dynamics of bureaucracy, the sociology of religion, and so on and on) and we can begin to understand how profoundly the young Parsons was influenced.

This is not to say that Parsons did not make good use of his time at Heidelberg to study other theorists besides Weber. He involved himself with the works of contemporary European social scientists as well as classical works of economics and philosophy. But it was the shadow of Max Weber which most strongly hovered over what Parsons learned in Germany.

After returning to the United States, Parsons arranged to continue with doctoral work at the University of Heidelberg. While he taught economics for a year at Amherst, he wrote a dissertation on "The Concept of Capitalism in Recent German Literature" and studied for major examinations in economic theory and sociological theory. He returned to Germany in the summer of 1927 to complete his doctorate. That fall he began teaching at Harvard as an instructor in economics.

Parsons' Theory of Social Action

Parsons went to Harvard in 1927 as much to study as to teach. He was among the most junior of faculty members when he began to work there, first as an instructor in economics and later as a teacher of sociology. Nevertheless, he enjoyed the chance to be among the great American economists then at Harvard, especially men such as Frank W. Taussig and Joseph A. Schumpeter. His own grasp of classical economics was enhanced by in-depth studies of the works of others, such as the late British economist, Alfred R. Marshall. His interest in the work of the great Italian economist and sociologist, Vilfredo Pareto, was spurred by contacts with Lawrence J. Henderson, who shared Pareto's enthusiasm for systems thinking and took a special interest in the career of Parsons.

In his European studies Parsons had not had occasion to deal with some of the currents then rising to prominence in American social science. That now was no longer feasible. As he later recalled,

> Returning to this country I found behaviorism so rampant that anyone who believed in the scientific validity of the interpretation of subjective states of mind was often held to be fatuously naïve. Also rampant was what I called "empiricism," namely the idea that scientific knowledge was a total reflection of the "reality out there," and even selection was alleged to be illegitimate.

Such influences Parsons clearly resisted. He charted his own theoretical course into what he came to call "analytical realism." The elements of such a theory are inherently abstract rather than directly empirical, but these abstractions should not be arbitrarily chosen. Rather they are to be founded on the study of real phenomena.[3]

When Parsons went to Harvard it had no department of sociology. He was, however, active in promoting such sociology courses as were offered. In 1930, the well-known Pitirim A. Sorokin came to Harvard as its first sociology professor, and the following year Sorokin headed the newly established department of sociology. Parsons then became an instructor for this new department and helped to develop sociology as a recognized discipline at Harvard.

It was not until 1936 that Parsons was made a member of Harvard's regular faculty. Nearing the end of nine years as a tutor and instructor, he was beginning to look elsewhere for continuing his career. Sorokin, his chairman, was apparently untroubled by this, for he had a rather low opinion of Parsons' work. However, other Harvard faculty members pushed to support a permanent appointment for Parsons, and Sorokin went along with the request. This led to Parsons' appointment as an assistant professor, with the promise of further promotion in two more years. He had finally established himself at Harvard, which was to be his academic base for the rest of his career.

For at least two years before he joined Harvard's permanent faculty, Parsons had been working on his first book (beyond his translations of Weber's work), and this was a factor in the decision to promote him.

When finally published in 1937, this book, *The Structure of Social Action*, provided support for Parsons' stature as a sociological theorist of the first rank. He showed himself well informed on the writings of other theorists. Especially did he draw on works by Vilfredo Pareto, the Italian economist and sociologist; Émile Durkheim, the French sociologist; and Max Weber, his favorite German theorist. From them he gained a common core of insights that he was able formulate into a theory of his own about basic social processes.[4]

How was social order possible, given the range of freedom that humans have to choose their own actions? This was a key question for Parsons. He raised it not to promote a particular pattern of social order, but rather to deal with the question about the fundamental properties of any social order. His central concept was that of "social action," and he was concerned to show how the forces of human society could be an ordered part of the ongoing patterns of behavior shown by individuals.

"Social action," for Parsons, involved not just raw behavior, but rather the meaningful actions of persons toward one another. Social actions have meanings and significance for the persons involved, and these meanings are not directly given as empirical data. Rather, they must be grasped through a theoretical understanding of the purposes and motives of the actors. This leads to the view that human actions are fundamentally voluntary, for they are not so much coerced by others as they are chosen to support the purposes of the individual who is the focus of action.

But social actions are not just assertions of individual wills. They are always conditioned by interaction with others. The conditions of human interaction give the fundamental directions for actions of individuals, and these conditions provide the basis of social order. The bedrock of human society consists of people acting together with one another in their groups and institutional settings.

Although not widely read immediately, within a few years *The Structure of Social Action* had established Parsons as a significant figure among American sociological theorists. In a remarkable achievement of theoretical synthesis he had assimilated the work of others into the framework of a new theory.

Harvard's Leading Sociologist

The ability of Talcott Parsons to provide synthesis for the work of others also showed itself in his academic leadership at Harvard. As soon as he was part of its sociology program, he was heavily involved with the unusually able graduate students that were attracted to Harvard and then went forth to become leaders of sociology at other institutions. He also developed good relations with other faculty members, both in sociology and in other fields. Shortly after when, in 1942, Sorokin asked to end his duties as the sociology department chair, Parsons replaced him. As he did so, however, it was with the understanding that he could pursue his ideas for a reorganization of social science units, which Parsons finally accomplished in 1946.

Together with such scholars as psychologists Gordon Allport and Henry Murray and the anthropologist Clyde Kluckhohn, Parsons planned for a combined social science department. Thus was the Department of Social Relations formed by the Harvard sociologists, clinical and social psychologists, and cultural anthropologists. Parsons was chairman of this new department, continuing in this role for its first ten years. This department soon became a center for exciting interdisciplinary developments, many of them led by Parsons himself.

Parsons' second main contribution to sociological theory, *The Social System*, was published in 1951. This expanded beyond *The Structure of Social Action* in discussing more fully the ways frameworks for human interaction are systematically organized. Chief among these forms of organization are social systems, which rest on patterns of shared norms among groups. But there are also other cross-cutting forms of organization that deserve to be recognized, especially personality systems (based on the continuity of individuals) and cultural systems (based on the continuity of norms).[5]

Also in 1951 came *Toward a General Theory of Action*. For this work, Edward Shils joined Parsons to lead an interdisciplinary exploration of ideas that had emerged from Parsons' work. Later in the 1950s were evident other significant fruits of collaboration led by Parsons. These included *Working Papers in the Theory of Action* (with Shils and Robert Bales in 1953), *Family, Socialization, and Interaction Process* (with Bales and others in 1955), and *Economy and Society* (with Neil J. Smelser in 1956). In these, Parsonian theory was widely applied to the functioning of small groups, to families, to personality development, and to the economy. What was becoming known as "structural-functional theory"—with Parsons its leading exponent—seemed to have risen to become the dominant theory in American social science by the end of the 1950s.[6]

The Rise and Fall of Structural-Functional Theory

Functional analysis has had a long history in the social sciences. It drew especially on the work of anthropologists and sociologists which looked at human society as a network of forces acting together in providing a fundamental unity among social institutions. More specifically, functionalism examines the consequences of particular ways of doing things for other parts of a society. What does a particular practice or belief system do to help in the integration of the larger framework of society? This question represents the central theme in functional analysis—how the parts of society are integrated into their larger pattern.

Pioneers in functional analysis included anthropologists Bronislaw Malinowski and A. R. Radcliffe-Brown and the great French sociologist Émile Durkheim. Parsons drew on all of these for his work on social systems. In addition, Parsons incorporated into his thinking the analysis of systems (including physical systems and living systems) of such theorists as Vilfredo Pareto and Lawrence J. Henderson. His own theories came to emphasize the way social systems are integrated. But social systems (viewed as patterns in the behavior of groups) are not the only systems involved in the functioning of human society. Individual motives are critical elements in the way social forms are developed (Parsons here became especially influenced by psychoanalysis), as are the patterns of norms found in any given cultural system. Society, from this perspective, is always a finely tuned system of interrelationships in which the parts are closely tied together.

Parsons included such central ideas of functional analysis and provided special conceptual systems to express the way social systems functioned. "Structural-functional theory" came to represent not only the general mode of functional analysis but also the conceptual tools that Parsons and his associates formulated. These included such features as the "pattern variables" (dichotomous ideal types applied to the general analyses of social action) and a variety of other concepts which helped to discuss the functional imperatives of social systems.

Parsons held that a series of abstract dichotomies can describe both the way individuals select their actions and how their systems of action develop and form social institutions. These "pattern variables" can be summarized into five questions posing the dilemmas of action in terms of ideal types:

1. Does the orientation of the actor incline toward specificity or diffuseness? For example, is the relationship to another person simply focused on the immediate situation, or does it include broad considerations about the meaning of this person to oneself?
2. Does the orientation of the actor incline toward affectivity or affective neutrality? For example, is the relationship with another person with, or without, a great deal of emotional involvement?

3.   Is the context of action to be seen in universalistic or particularistic terms? For example, are the standards to be applied to behavior matters of general consensus or are they based on the specific individuals involved?
4.   Is the context of action to be seen in terms of ascription or achievement? For example, are they defined by general qualities with which individuals are endowed, or are they defined by the way individuals perform their activities?
5.   Does the orientation of action involve primarily self-orientation or collectivity-orientation? For example, is one to focus on his or her interests as an individual, or are group interests and goals involved?

Parsons held that all social relationships can be categorized in terms of such basic variables as these, and he extended them broadly in the analysis of all forms of social systems—even to characterizing entire human societies.[7]

Parsons and his associates also developed a framework for viewing the functional imperatives of a social system. Every social system—from a brief interpersonal relationship to the much larger system of a society as a whole—must meet four fundamental needs. These may be summarized as (1) adaptation, (2) goal-attainment, (3) integration, and (4) latent pattern-maintenance and tension management. Together these may be referred to as the "AGIL" scheme, based on the first letter for each basic function. Adaptation to an environment, goal attainment within that environment, integration of parts within the system, and maintenance of basic normative patters—these were for Parsons the key requirements of any social system. These also therefore became key terms with which structural-functionalism sought to analyze social systems of all types.[8]

As we have seen, Parsons was widely considered as America's leading social theorist by the end of the 1950s. Then came the 1960s, and the dominance of structural-functional theory ended. It became seen by many as a pretentious form of a basically conservative ideology. The great forces of social change—so apparent in the 1960s—did not seem to be so well explained by structural-functional theories. Social scientists had begun to place more emphasis on conflict theories, social exchange models, and other ways of picturing the less-than-complete social order that seemed to prevail.

By 1970, a new sociology department emerged at Harvard. The Department of Social Relations, with which Parsons had been so strongly identified, was to be no more. His official retirement came three years later. However, Parsons continued an active career, and his later years saw the production of social theory significantly different in its emphasis from that which had established his reputation. Much more was he concerned with political processes (as in *Politics and Social Structure*, published in 1969) and in processes of social change (as in *The System of Modern Societies*, published in 1971, and *The Evolution of Societies*, published in 1977).[9]

Parsons saw modern society as emerging out of an increasing capacity of environmental adaptation. Societies become modified structurally with successful adaptation. The parts of society become increasingly differentiated, and this allows them to develop greater flexibility in the ways they adapt. With this flexibility comes an increasing capacity for the society to include a wide range of kinds of institutions and groups of people. In modern multi-group societies such as those of the United States and Western Europe, the forces of economic development and democratization have reached impressive levels of complex development. But these forces are not unique to the West. Parsons held indeed that "the forces that have transformed the societal community of the United States and promise to continue to transform it are not peculiar to this one society but permeate the whole modern—and 'modernizing'—world."[10]

In the spring of 1979, Talcott Parsons returned to Germany for appearances at Heidelberg and Munich. He was first honored at Heidelberg on the occasion of the fiftieth anniversary of his doctorate there. Then on May 8 he had just finished a lecture at Munich University when, back with his wife at their hotel, he suffered a stroke. He died that evening.

The Province of Theory

For John Dewey, theory was never an end in itself. It was part of the stuff of human experience, and he resisted giving it a province of its own. For him, the search to treat theoretical contemplation as fundamentally different from the experience of our everyday lives was one of the perennial banes of philosophy.

Talcott Parsons had no such qualms about being a theorist. Abstract theory seemed to be in his life's blood, and he sought to elevate the work of theory building to become the highest calling for social science. Being a theorist was not so much a fundamental philosophical position for him as the natural way he went about his work as a social scientist.

For Parsons, theory derived in principle from the empirical world—but often quite indirectly. While always fundamentally about the world studied by other social scientists, his theories were of such a degree of abstraction and generality that they often seemed to constitute a world of their own. Indeed, he came to see a reality for his central concepts which was more than forming convenient categories of reference. Add to this his rather turgid style of writing—recognized as such by both his admirers and detractors—and you have the main ingredients of Parsons' style of grand theory. Parsons was both a theorist who could seem to mystify the normal social world behind a maze of verbiage, and a theorist who could bring together brilliant insights of others into a new synthesis.

Inevitably, there is the question of Parsons' ideological preconceptions. Many have seen his functionalism as inherently conservative, with a priority given to seeing how society has become what it is rather than to emphasize how changes come about. Actually, his later works seem to devote a great deal more attention to social change than his earlier, better known writings. But the conservative impression remained attached to him to an extent that he found puzzling, for he was not generally an advocate for conservative social causes. A number of the most recent analyses of his thought have indeed emphasized him as a "theorist of modernity" and a proponent of modern democratic values.[11]

Parsons did not deny that his own personal experiences affected the things he studied. For example, his religious background may have, as some have suggested, been an important influence on his work. He did not deny this. But rather than see this area as a matter of personal religious views, the study of religion was for him "a focus of a continuing attempt to understand the balance of the roles of rational and nonrational components in human action." It was, in other words, seen as an opportunity to seek for new theoretical insights about the fundamental integration of social systems rather than as a framework to express personal beliefs.[12]

Social science had been described by Parsons' hero Max Weber as a vocation where one is duty bound not to let personal values intrude directly into scholarly work. In a similar manner Talcott Parsons saw social theory as his calling. As much as possible, he felt, ideological commitments should be set aside and social theory pursued as a study for its own sake.

8

Kenneth Boulding: Economist Without Boundaries

From the Dirty Streets of Liverpool

Born there on January 18, 1910, Kenneth Boulding grew up on Seymour Street, near the center of Liverpool, England. He later recalled,

> It was a dirty city, a product of the coal age. Often in the winter we could hardly see the other side of the street through the black fog. Buildings were all black, sometimes even festooned with soot. Clothes and curtains got dirty overnight in a constantly losing battle against the dirt. But I took all this for granted.[1]

Although his father made a living as a plumber, the family faced a constant economic struggle. They lived modestly but respectably; and Kenneth, an only child, was showered with love and attention. He grew up to become a tall but awkward young man, with social skills hampered by a severe stuttering problem. Strongly religious, the Bouldings made their Methodist chapel a core part of their lives. Boulding was to maintain a strong religious faith throughout his life, though he later moved from his Methodist roots to become a Quaker.

His parents saw that Kenneth had the best education they could provide. He took to his schooling with great energy and success. "I was a very bright boy, and particularly good at passing examinations," he has said. In his secondary education he emphasized mathematics and science, and this led to a scholarship for study at Oxford. After one year there in chemistry, he changed to study philosophy, politics, and economics.[2]

Though deeply motivated by his studies at Oxford, Kenneth did not find the social life there pleasant. "Even though I gradually made a circle of friends at Oxford, mainly from among the outcasts, I never felt either accepted or at home," he said. Among the liabilities he carried to Oxford were "my Liverpool accent, speech impediment, and Methodist teetotalism."

Finishing his undergraduate work at Oxford in 1931, Boulding stayed on for a year of graduate studies. Then he applied for, and was awarded, a Commonwealth Fellowship for study in America. This brought him to the University of Chicago where, in contrast to his experience at Oxford, he found immediate acceptance. He joined vigorously into the intellectual life there—both in his contacts with the faculty and with fellow students living at the new International House.

Called back to Liverpool by the death of his father, Boulding faced the daunting problem of trying to settle family financial accounts. Discovering that debts exceeded remaining funds, he found that he "learned more economics" than in "any other ten days in my life." Boulding brought his mother back with him to the United States while he pursued further studies briefly at Harvard and Chicago. But financial considerationswere significant in leading him to end his graduate work without finishing a doctorate.[3]

Back in Britain in 1934, Boulding felt extremely fortunate to find a job teaching economics at Edinburgh University. He and his mother were there for three years. The intellectual climate was, in Boulding's expressed view, "bleak"—especially compared to what he had known at Chicago. However, he continued to develop his career as an economist at Edinburgh and enjoyed being part of the Friends meeting there.

While at a world conference of the Society of Friends in Philadelphia in 1937, Boulding heard of a teaching opening at Colgate University in upstate New York. He applied for the position, and was warmly accepted. From this point on he and his mother became residents of the United States.

Boulding had published his first article in the field of economics while a student at Oxford. Several other articles followed during his graduate work and three years at Edinburgh. While at Colgate, Boulding wrote his *Economic Analysis*, which was published in 1941. This book also came out in three later editions, becoming one of the most read textbooks available for beginning students of economics.[4]

But economics was not Boulding's only interest. Active in the Society of Friends, he wrote several small books expressing pacifist views. The first, *Paths of Glory*, was published in 1937. He also wrote poetry, with the "Naylor Sonnets" (published in 1945 with the title of *There is a Spirit*) becoming his best-known work.

It was through his involvement in Quaker activities that he met the woman who was to become his wife. He later summarized this event as follows:

In May 1941 at a Friends Quarterly Meeting in Syracuse I found myself sitting almost knee to knee with a disturbing presence. Her name was Elise Bjorn-Hansen. She was Norwegian by birth, just about to join the Society of Friends. We were engaged in eighteen days and married in two months.

Elise later finished her doctorate in sociology and became a leading scholar in that field. She and Kenneth had five children and many years of close companionship. With his gift for saying much in a few words, Kenneth described their two-career marriage as follows:

We have both written a lot of books, have been president of this and that, and have had a marvelously good life.[5]

A Solid Base in Economics

Kenneth Boulding's teachers had quickly identified him as an unusually promising student of economics. He showed himself to have a critical mind about central ideas in the field by questioning in print the views of his well known professor at Chicago, Frank Knight. In response he received Knight's admiration and also serious recognition among other economists who read their published exchange. During his brief time at Harvard, he discussed key ideas freely with Joseph Schumpeter, one of the world's most famous economists. He was clearly a young economist to watch.

Boulding's first book project was a general work in economic theory. In this he focused on the dynamics of the business firm in achieving an equilibrium within the larger framework of the economy as a whole. Its title was to be *Investment and Production: The Theory of a Single Economic Process.* Unfortunately, he was unable to find a publisher for this work.

Boulding then began his textbook, *Economic Analysis*, which established his fame. In this work he applied a fresh approach to the field, organizing the subject around tools of analysis. He started with the basic concepts of supply and demand and applied them to simple cases, then he introduced more complex variables into the framework. He also included some of the latest economic ideas then entering the field. All in all, it was a summary of what he had learned about economics, presented in a form that could be readily grasped by a beginning student.[6]

A more technical work by Boulding came out in 1950 under the title of *A Reconstruction of Economics*. In this he attempted to present some of his most original ideas. He focused especially upon a theory about capital formation and maintenance, which led him to view consumption in a manner different from that of most economists. He expressed his key point in this way:

> Once the emphasis is laid on assets rather than on income it becomes clear that there is a vital distinction between the enjoyment of assets and their consumption—that is, destruction. Consumption, and therefore production and income, are then seen as quantities to be minimized rather than to be maximized in the interests of maximum enjoyment.

In other words, the primary aim—both for the firm and for society as a whole—should be the enhancement of assets rather than their consumption. This was an idea which he carried further in later work beyond economics in which he posed the interests of environmental preservation (for what he came to call "spaceship earth") as opposed to those of maximum economic growth and development. Clearly, Boulding was searching for economic tools that would serve human ends other than a simple desire for enhanced production or "prosperity."[7]

In this book and in other writings Boulding put forward what he called his "bathtub theorem." Drawing on a basic conception of John Maynard Keynes that the accumulation of capital at any point in time is equal to its production minus consumption, he suggested that one might conceive of capital assets as a body of water—such as in a bathtub. We can turn down the "faucet" under conditions of recession and unemployment, thus lowering the capital intake, pull the "plug" to expand consumption, or knock out a hole in the side in a fit of destruction (war, for instance). All of these affect the water available (or capital stocks). Generally the price system automatically regulates valves which control the inflow and outflow of assets, though Boulding was enough of a Keynesian to hold that under certain conditions special policies of governments may be needed to provide outside regulation.

Responses of other economists were quite mixed to *A Reconstruction of Economics*. Most were not ready to change their concepts in the manner he suggested. Part of the criticisms of others dealt with technical details. A more basic criticism concerned the general direction he thought economics should go. As one economist expressed this, "It was his effort to move modern economics into the general systems area, and it didn't take; the profession went off in other directions."[8]

Boulding wrote other books intended to include a broader audience beyond economists. One of these, *The Economics of Peace*, an attempt to relate economic principles to issues of war and peace, was published in 1945. Though it received some favorable reviews, it was not widely read. About this book Boulding has said, "It was never an uproarious success."[9]

Later Boulding gave a non-technical introduction to economic thinking in the form of a little book titled *The Skills of the Economist* (published in 1958). In this lucid review Boulding emphasized that economics provides a very special way of looking at the world. It focuses not on human behavior in any direct sense, but rather on "commodities" (which are given value because of their scarcity) and how they may be exchanged. This is a highly abstract perspective, but one with a rich array of possibilities for the analysis of how people (in individual firms or in society as a whole) may maximize their interests. But, again, this is not a complete picture of the world.[10]

Although economics provides only one way of looking at human activities, Boulding showed that it can be extended far beyond the traditional role of business decision making. Its extension soon raises questions that are of an ethical nature. Here economists and the public policies they advocate can give us only part of our answers. They help us in rational decision making, but many of our basic questions take us to seek values that lie beyond rational calculations. We are motivated by faith as well as reason, and our forms of faith may be shaped by what Boulding calls "the heroic ethic." He ends the book on a very personal note concerning the kind of ethic that may be most useful for our age:

> I am convinced that pagan heroism, as represented by Hitler at its worst and by Churchill at its best, can only lead to destruction. All the noblest elements of man are pressed into the service of the pagan state—his courage, his self-sacrifice, and his science. They serve but to accentuate the tragic dynamics of mutual destruction. That man may be saved from his own power I look to another kind of heroism: the heroism of the terrible meek, of those who have seen the vision of perfect, not partial love. I look, that is, to the heroism of the Nazarene.[11]

From Pacifism to Peace Research

When Kenneth and Elise Boulding married in the summer of 1941, he was beginning work at a new job as an economist with the League of Nations. For this the Bouldings established their home at Princeton, New Jersey, and Kenneth began working on analyses of European agriculture.

Then came December 7 and America's involvement in World War II. As most Americans were promoting a maximum war effort, the Bouldings saw this as a time to try to stop what they saw as madness. One result was their drawing up of a statement, "A Call to Disarm," which they intended to circulate privately. Before it was sent out, Kenneth showed it to his supervisors, who warned him that he would be fired from his job if such a statement was openly circulated. The Bouldings sent out their letter anyway, and Kenneth submitted his resignation to the League of Nations.

Kenneth accepted a teaching job at Fisk University, beginning in the fall of 1942, and a year later the Bouldings moved to Ames, Iowa, where he taught economics at Iowa State University while Elise studied sociology there. They remained at Ames for most of the next six years (with one year away at McGill University, Montreal), continuing their scholarly work and involvement in Quaker activities.

Although strongly identified with America, Boulding was not a citizen until December 1948. As a permanent resident he was forced to face the military draft. He sought the status of a conscientious objector, and was fully prepared to accept prison rather than to become a soldier. But then he failed to pass his physical examination. Later he found his request for citizenship held up by his refusal to pledge a willingness to take up arms to defend his new country. It took a court decision to clear the way for him to receive citizenship papers. When he finally received them, he was overjoyed, for he loved his new country. He saw this as "one of the happiest moments of my life, and I hope I can prove worthy of the trust implied."[12]

The following year, 1949, Boulding became a professor at the University of Michigan, and the Bouldings remained at Ann Arbor (except for limited periods away) for the next eighteen years. At Ann Arbor they continued their work with the Quakers and provided other forms of support for pacifist causes. More important, however, was Boulding's work in the peace research movement. He, with others at the University of Michigan, became leaders of this new field.

During 1954-55 Boulding was a fellow at the Center for Advanced Study in the Behavioral Sciences at Palo Alto, California. In interaction with other leading scholars there, he considered how research might be more effectively focused on questions about war and peace. After his return to Michigan he led a group which fostered interdisciplinary exchange around the general subject of conflict. Together they started a new journal, the *Journal of Conflict Resolution*, and established the Center for the Study of Conflict Resolution. The University of Michigan thus became the leader of this developing new field for interdisciplinary research and graduate education.

Before "peace research" had become widely recognized, Boulding had made important contributions in this field. His *Economics of Peace*, published in 1945, provides one example. However, with the stimulus of the Center for the Study of Conflict Resolution, he expanded his efforts in this direction. The most notable results were the books *Conflict and Defense*, published in 1962, and *Disarmament and the Economy* (co-edited with Emile Benoit), published the following year.[13]

Conflict and Defense was Boulding's attempt to develop a general theory of conflict processes. Patterns of action and reaction in human conflict may be submitted to systematic analysis in a manner similar to the way meteorologists study air currents to understand the onset of storms. Boulding presents several ways of looking at the basic dynamics of conflict, including the rational models of the theory of games and the gross patterns of epidemiological models. Especially original is his application of what economists have called the "viability of the firm" (to study in what markets a firm may be effective) to more general phenomena of conflict. His use of this concept helps to understand the conditions under which successful defenses might be mounted. to stabilize a conflict.

Although many at the time were pessimistic about what might be the economic effects of disarmament, Boulding sought to show in *Disarmament and the Economy* that such effects could be successfully managed. The editors summarized in the preface the nature of their contribution in this work:

> We are under no illusions that disarmament is easy or close, or that the economic adjustments are the major problem involved. The political problems of disarmament are the most difficult and the most important, and the economic problems will rise in importance only as the political problems are solved. It is essential, however, to know that we can solve the economic problems concerned; otherwise, our fears in this regard, even though they are below the surface, may operate as a serious handicap in our efforts to solve the political problem.[14]

In 1963, Elise Boulding began editing the International Peace Research Newsletter, and the Bouldings were active in peace research activities throughout the rest of their lives.

Boulding never outgrew his pacifist roots. The ethic of love was ever central in his religious faith, and he was always suspicious of the arbitrary power of the modern state. But peace, he held, could develop more effectively from knowledge than from sentiment. The knowledge that could come from a systematic study of social forces was as important for resolving conflict, he believed, as having one's heart in the right place.

Beyond All Boundaries

The development of general systems theory was another main product of Boulding's 1954-55 year at the Center for Advanced Study in the

Behavioral Sciences. Boulding, Ludwig von Bertalanffy and Anatol Rapoport were among those advocates of interdisciplinary work who developed a special theory group focused on the study of the interaction of systems (physical, biological, and social) with their environments. This group emerged into the Society for General Systems Research in December of 1954. Boulding served as its first president.

At the conclusion of his year in California, general systems theory was very much upon Boulding's mind as he and Elise made plans to return to Michigan. During a period of nine days in August of 1955, he dictated a wide-ranging commentary on the state of human knowledge which was to become one of his most influential books. This was *The Image*, published in 1956. Here was a theory of knowledge and behavior centered on the perceptions that people hold about their world. These perceptions include effects of individual filters based on personal experience, but they also include the common meanings that are the legacy of group experience. How such meanings, individual and collective, affect behavior is the central subject matter of the book.[15]

Although *The Image* is focused on processes of human perception, Boulding suggested that there is something similar going on in other kinds of systems. Physical and biological systems have feedback mechanisms that help them adjust to their environments, often with what might be represented as accumulated experience. In a very broad sense, non-human organisms and even physical systems come to "know" what is going on in the environment and use that "knowledge" as a basis of selective action. But our knowledge about such processes is hampered by our tendency to carve up reality into our special disciplines. Perhaps a new discipline is now needed to study the emergence of images in whatever form they may be found. He suggested the outlines of what might become the new science of "eiconics," which should draw upon biology, philosophy, psychology, and the full range of the social sciences. Eiconics did not become generally recognized as a new science, but general systems theory continued to grow in its attempts to integrate various fields of human knowledge.

The Image was not the first book to show Boulding's broad interdisciplinary interests, and it certainly was not the last. Just before the Bouldings left for their year in California, *The Organizational Revolution* was published. In this book Boulding took note of the great variety of organizations which emerged in the late nineteenth century, and he sought in the basic nature of organizations clues as to how they might grow or divide. A later work in which Boulding made even more clear his general systems orientation was *The World as a Total System*. In this culminating example of his systems thinking, he sought to apply all the main elements of systems—from physical systems to those of human communication and evaluation—to the world as a whole.[16]

In 1967 Kenneth and Elise moved to Boulder, Colorado, where both were offered faculty appointments at the University of Colorado. Thereafter he retained Colorado as his primary home, though he traveled widely over the world for visiting professorships and other lectures. Cancer led to his death on March 18, 1993.

Boulding never ceased being an economist. However, his later contributions increasingly examined the wider social context of the science of economics and ranged freely into other fields. An example of his broadening of the range of economics was what he called "grants economics." He pointed out that important economic phenomena include gifts and one-way transfers as well as market exchanges. He sought to develop the analysis of this area both as a new segment of the field of economics and as a way of exploring the integrative processes of social systems. Also, within the broad field of welfare economics was another area, explicitly focused on processes of evaluating economic outcomes, which Boulding helped develop under the name of "the economics of human betterment."[17]

In 1989 Boulding published *Three Faces of Power*, a book which brought together a number of the important threads of the final part of his career. General systems theory, peace studies, and economic and political analysis were all woven into the fabric of this comprehensive theory of human power. In this book he distinguished three main kinds of power in human society: threat power, productive power, and integrative power. Threat power resides especially in its ability to destroy, and is seen most clearly in political and military affairs. Productive power rests on the production and exchange of goods, and is especially subject to economic analyses. Finally, there is integrative power, the power of solidifying people in their social institutions based on their psychological identifications and voluntary commitments. Boulding does not hesitate to use words such as "love" and "respect" in relation to the social bases of integrative power. Although none of these three forms of power can stand completely alone without some elements of the other two, it is a primary thesis of Boulding's that integrative power is in some sense the most basic. Neither threat power nor economic power can achieve very much, he asserts, in the absence of social legitimacy for those seeking to exercise power. Such legitimacy is one of the most important aspects of integrative power. Summarizing this idea in the final sentence of the book, he asserts, "The stick, the carrot, and the hug may all be necessary, but the greatest of these is the hug."[18]

Transcending Social Theory

For John Dewey social theory was a product of social experience, rooted in turn in the human adjustment to a natural world. Talcott Parsons was less broadly philosophical about the roots of social theory, but he clearly saw abstract theory as the center of his life's work. Kenneth Boulding is more difficult to classify as a social theorist than either Dewey or Parsons. Boulding was an economist who made important theoretical contributions to his discipline—for which his colleagues honored him as president of the American Economics Association in 1968. But he was much more than an economist. He was one of the most general of social science theorists, with his work covering a wide array of topics. But he was more than an economist, social scientist, or scientist. He was also a poet and humanist, and a deeply religious man.[19]

With his breadth of interests and the enormous volume of his writings, it is inevitable that the quality of Boulding's work was uneven. Other social scientists were often frustrated by the cavalier way he treated their special fields of knowledge. But Boulding's brilliance also often came through, sometimes when least expected.

For Kenneth Boulding social theory always pointed to something beyond the present concerns of analysis. He loved to form new abstractions, then try to test how widely they might apply; but he also found great personal satisfaction in the concrete world of everyday life.

Ultimately, Boulding's concern was as much of an ethical nature as that of a scientist. Cynthia Kerman, his biographer, has called him a "missionary of reality images." She describes him as constantly seeking the forms of knowledge which would enhance "an ethical system built on a view of the world as a community." His ethical concerns were part of the background of his great works of theory, and the central theme of a common humanity was repeatedly affirmed in his work.[20]

Part 4

Reformers

9

Gunnar and Alva Myrdal:
Social Science as Social Engineering

A Romantic Beginning

During a vacation, three students were on a bicycle trip through central Sweden. On June 5, 1919, they stopped at the farm of Albert Reimer, who allowed them to spend the night in his barn. Early the next morning he invited these strangers to the house for early morning coffee. This is how the farmer's daughter, Alva Reimer, met Gunnar Myrdal.

Alva was a shy young blonde woman with bright blue eyes. Born January 31, 1902, she was the oldest of five children in the Reimer family. She was seventeen when she met the young Myrdal. Despite her deep love of books, she had not been able to attend the local "gymnasium" (as Swedes called their secondary schools) because it then accepted only males. Her mother was strongly opposed to her leaving home to study elsewhere, so she stayed with the family and completed a business training course, then became employed in a local government office. Only later that year would she begin her secondary schooling through the special efforts of her father, who helped to arrange private schooling for a group of young women.

Gunnar Myrdal was then a law student at the University of Stockholm. Born December 6, 1898, he was just twenty when he met Alva. Though from a region of the country considered by many to be backward, Gunnar's self confidence in his own intellect was clearly justified by his school achievements. He loved to explore ideas with faculty members and fellow students and viewed himself as becoming part of the intellectual elite of his country.

Gunnar's self confidence may have shown a temporary pause when he first met Alva, but her obvious interest spurred him on. To her he seemed knowledgeable about everything, and she was eager to share in his genius. To him she seemed to be an unusually well-read young woman, and soon they were talking about contemporary novels and evolutionary biology.

Gunnar returned to the Reimer farm so he could continue meeting this remarkable young woman. Then he invited her to join him in a bike trip, and much to his surprise she accepted. Her mother was away from home at that time, and she misled her father by talk about visiting a girlfriend. Several days later, they visited at the home of Gunnar's parents, and only after that did they venture to express physical affection toward one another. Then, as Gunnar would later express it, "we lived in a happy world of love."[1]

As they continued their education, Gunnar and Alva saw each other when able. In 1922, Alva began work at the University of Stockholm, which she was able to complete two years later. Her studies emphasized the history of religion, Scandinavian languages, and the history of literature. At the time she considered the possibility of becoming a librarian. Gunnar received his degree in 1923 and began the private practice of law. Marriage came in the fall of 1924. It was officially marked by a simple private ceremony with only two friends present as witnesses. Both Alva and Gunnar saw this as marking their independence from the families into which they had been born, and none of the parents of either the bride or groom were invited.

Economics and Activism

Gunnar Myrdal found himself bored by his early work as a lawyer, and he considered how his talents might be better served. He had a good mind for mathematics, the study of economic issues had always interested him, and he found the prospects of the life of a scholar attractive. Furthermore, the University of Stockholm had an excellent economics faculty, led by one of the great neoclassical scholars of that time, Gustav Cassel. Given all of these factors, plus the active encouragement of his young wife, Gunnar took up the study of economics.

Gunnar soon mastered his new field, and the Myrdals came to be close personal friends of Cassel and his wife. Professor Cassel became something of an intellectual father to Gunnar, showing the kind of personal qualities and broad learning that the fledgling economist most admired. Cassel in turn found Gunnar to be the ideal student—brilliant in his grasp of subject matter, serious in his scholarship, and with a generally pleasant disposition. Extending some of Cassel's work with price theory for his thesis, Gunnar Myrdal was awarded the doctorate in 1927.

Encouraged by his professor to stay on at the University of Stockholm, Gunnar Myrdal soon made a reputation there as one of Europe's most promising young economists. When Cassel retired in 1933, Myrdal replaced him as Lars Hjerta Professor of Economics. By then he had begun to question many of the assumptions of classical economics, but Cassel still gave him his blessing. At the installation ceremony the elder scholar embraced his thirty-five-year-old replacement, saying "You are the most dangerous man in Sweden, but I'm proud to have you as my successor."[2]

That Cassel might consider his onetime protégé as "dangerous" reflected the increasingly critical stance Myrdal was taking in regard to classical economics. The young scholar was not an opponent criticizing the field from outside, but as an insider who questioned the very foundations of the field. In 1928, Myrdal had given a series of lectures in which he suggested that there were hidden social and political biases behind the most "objective" presentations of economics. Two years later this work was published as *The Political Element in the Development of Economic Theory*. He here pointed to "quasi-scientific dogmas in the political sphere" which "serve as powerful obstructions to clear and realistic thinking in practical questions." He suggested, for example, that a philosophy of natural law gave an overly ideal picture of how markets in capitalistic systems are regulated. He held that a broader picture of society, including social values other than purely economic motives, was necessary if economists were to understand the most important features of their economic systems. He especially turned to politics as playing a critical role in the way economic systems operate. "All institutional factors which determine the structure of the market," he said, "can be changed, if those interested in the change have enough political power."[3]

Another example of Gunnar Myrdal's pioneering work in economics was his *Monetary Equilibrium*, published in 1931. He here considered how prices may be affected by historical changes and popular expectations which operate in ways other than through the classical conceptions of supply and demand.

In the early years of their marriage Alva had no academic position, but she was able to pursue her studies less formally. Psychology became her central interest, and she became well read in this field. The Myrdal home became a center of freewheeling discussions among Stockholm intellectuals who dealt especially with political and social issues. Gunnar's sense of humor and sharp intelligence made him a natural center of these discussions. Though Alva was less likely to take the lead, she also showed herself to have an independent and well informed mind. Gunnar and Alva clearly had a high regard for each other's minds and each drew upon the other in their intellectual development. For example, Gunnar's broadening of interests in the field of economics, making it more subject to sociological and psychological factors, was to a large extent the result of Alva's influence.

Although Gunnar accepted the main tenets of feminism, he assumed that his own wife would be the one to deal with the main tasks of running the household. Also, he did not have an easy style for dealing with young children, and Alva took on the primary child-rearing responsibilities after their first child was born in 1927. Still, when Gunnar applied for a Rockefeller Foundation fellowship to study in America during the 1929-30 academic year, he made it a condition of his application that Alva would be awarded a similar grant. So both Gunnar and Alva spent an exciting year visiting American centers of learning. Gunnar made personal contact with "institutional economists," such as John R. Commons at the University of Wisconsin, who sought to draw out the social roots of economic phenomena. Alva became familiar with the most current work in social psychology and child development. Both were impressed with the dynamic nature of American society. Although the stock market crash of 1929 occurred shortly after their arrival and they saw the seriousness of America's economic crisis, their most general impressions about America were favorable.

After a year in America came a year at Geneva, Switzerland, where Gunnar taught at the Graduate Institute for International Studies while Alva studied early child development at the Jean-Jacques Rousseau Institute.

Two years away from Sweden had given the Myrdals new perspectives on their home country. They saw many ways that the Swedes could learn from other Europeans and from Americans. An article that Gunnar wrote in 1932 titled "The Dilemma of Social Policy" summed up his views on the need for economics to move beyond its classical traditions to welcome broader efforts at social engineering.

Within the context of Swedish politics, Gunnar and Alva were now ready for active involvement in the Swedish Social Democratic party. Since the end of the Great War, when universal suffrage came to Sweden, the socialist movement had been growing in its challenge to liberal, conservative, and agrarian parties. In the 1920s the Social Democrats become the largest single party, and in the early 1930s (fed by the economic crisis then being felt throughout the world) they became the dominant party. Gunnar Myrdal soon became a leading economic advisor for the government, and was elected to the senate as a Social Democrat in 1934. Alva, whose socialist ideals began in her early childhood, became an even more ardent supporter of reform programs of the Social Democrats.

In a cabin in the mountains of Norway during the summer of 1934, Alva and Gunnar wrote a book which was to make them famous. This book, *Kris i beholkningsfragan* (or "Crisis in the Population Question") soon became a Swedish best seller. It started by noting the problem of Sweden's declining birth rate, then the lowest in Europe. The possibilities of a declining population concerned many thoughtful Swedes, including the Myrdals. What was new in their work was the response they proposed. Rather than appealing to conservative family values to produce more children, they suggested that more modern attitudes and social welfare measures should be emphasized.

There was, the Myrdals held, a "cultural lag" between the rural roots of family ideals and the realities of modern urban life. What was needed was to make the institutions of the modern world more hospitable for families who bring children into the world. By dealing systematically with unemployment, low wages, poor housing, and inadequate child care facilities, they held that Sweden could both reverse its low birth rate and create a better world for all its citizens. Women's rights were to be respected and family planning encouraged. There should be no limitation in access to birth control information, nor should access to public child care facilities be limited by a lack of economic resources.

Their book, *Kris*, put the Myrdals at the center of Sweden's political debate. The stakes were no less than the establishment of the welfare state as a primary objective of political action. Gunnar and Alva accepted their roles as social activists and came to be leading architects of reform proposals. So well known were they as figures in the public debate that a new term was added to the Swedish language—"to myrdal" became a new way of referring to sexual intercourse.

As the Social Democrats made population issues of central political importance, other parties also expressed their concerns. The result was a Royal Population Commission, which included representatives of all major parties in a special effort to study the problems involved and make recommendations for legislative action. Gunnar Myrdal was appointed to this commission and soon became its leading figure. Meanwhile, Alva was pioneering in the field of early childhood education. In 1936 she helped to establish the Seminar for Social Pedagogy, which became Sweden's leading teacher training center for preschool education. Under her direction the seminar came to emphasize the forms of progressive education that John Dewey was leading in America, with social cooperation a key educational objective.

Both Gunnar and Alva were heavily involved in social reform in Sweden in 1937 when Gunnar received a surprising offer from America. It was an opportunity for work on a completely new problem, that of race relations in the United States. At first he politely declined the proposal, citing his commitments in Sweden. "These Americans are crazy," he said to his wife; but then the two of them thought more about the surprising proposal. As Gunnar later recalled, "we were sitting up in bed and I said to Alva, 'Perhaps we should do this thing at the end of our youth.'" This led them to discuss the possibilities anew, and the next day Gunnar sent off a cable to New York saying he was ready to consider the American offer.[4]

The "Dilemma" in America

During the early 1930s the Carnegie Corporation supported a number of small projects concerning American Negroes. This private foundation had been formed in 1911 by Andrew Carnegie "to promote the advancement and diffusion of knowledge," and its trustees often considered projects that might make a major impact upon society.

In 1935 one of its trustees pointed to the problems of Negroes in northern cities and suggested that a study of this subject be undertaken. In pursuing this idea, Frederick Keppel, the foundation's president, felt that a more ambitious study would be appropriate, one that would deal more generally with race relations in America. Gradually the idea was developed that a leading scholar or statesman might be supported to travel and study the "Negro problem" in America, then after a year or so of study write a report on the findings.

Much careful consideration of who might be invited to lead such a study had been given by Carnegie staff members and advisors before Gunnar Myrdal was approached. It was concluded that it should be someone from outside the United States who was not known to have strong views about racial matters. Also, a leading social scientist would be desirable, for the project now had been expanded to consist of a series of studies conducted within a period of two years. Finally, attention was directed to the young Swedish economist, and Keppel (who as Carnegie president was to be intimately involved in the project throughout its history) sent a letter to Myrdal in August of 1937 to assess his interest. A series of delicate negotiations followed which gave Myrdal generous financial incentives and a relatively free hand to supervise the project. Included in the plans were Carnegie support for Richard Sterner, a social statistician, to come from Sweden to assist Myrdal in his work and a special grant for Alva Myrdal to study at Columbia University.

On September 10, 1938, the Myrdals arrived in New York. Immediately they made a favorable impression on the Americans they met. Their appearance then has been described as follows:

> At thirty-six, Alva was a striking blond, fashionably dressed, quietly self-confident with a direct gaze and serious demeanor, always polite and seldom at a loss for words. Gunnar, at thirty-nine, was a dynamo with piercing blue eyes, a shock of light brown hair, and a mercurial temperament that alternated between playful banter and intense absorption in intellectual work. He was constantly erupting with ideas and questions about every aspect of American life.[5]

After a tour of the American South and a personal examination of the extensive literature on American race relations, Gunnar Myrdal wrote an outline for Keppel of general plans. He would concentrate more on contemporary racial problems than their historical development. He would also seek to study those matters that might be of greatest practical significance for developing public policies and social programs. Keppel encouraged him to proceed in this manner and gave generous support for specific studies recommended by Myrdal (who was to use not only his own research but that of many other specially commissioned studies).

Myrdal soon found that American race relations were more complicated than he had imagined. Both in his personal investigations and the more formal research he examined, he was struck with the difficulties of forming clear conclusions. It began to look like a project that could not be completed within the projected two years. A further complication was the onset of World War II.

When they came to America in 1938 the Myrdals had not expected a general war to be soon occurring in Europe. By mid-1940 much of Europe, including Denmark and Norway, had been engulfed by the German war machine, and the continuing neutrality of Sweden was severely strained. Under these circumstances, Gunnar and Alva felt a call to Sweden to help resist German pressures to undermine its political neutrality and to keep alive cultural ties to other Western democracies. They therefore returned to Sweden, leaving the American race relations study temporarily in the hands of others. Even though he had by then spent nearly two years on this project, Gunnar Myrdal still had no general framework within which his conclusions might be presented.

Gunnar and Alva used their experiences in America to help their fellow Swedes hold fast to their democratic values while surrounded by Nazi influences. In part they did this through a book of their essays which was published in 1941 as *Kontakt med Amerika* ("Contact with America"). Their reflections on what they had observed in the United States showed a strong admiration for the manner with which Americans faced their social problems. For example, in helping to explain the unity amid the diversity of American society, they said,

> America, ahead of every other country in the whole Western world, large or small, has a living system of expressed ideals for human cooperation which is unified, stable, and clearly formulated. The political belief system is not simply as among us, latent, unpracticed principles which—in degrees of compromise—find expression in the nation's laws and political order. [Rather, in America they are principles that] have been made conscious and articulate in all social levels.

They termed this set of principles "the American Creed." When he returned to his project in America, Gunnar Myrdal was to made central use of this set of ideas about America.[6]

In Sweden Gunnar Myrdal was often reminded of his unfinished work in the United States. His friend Sterner, who had stayed with the project in America, pointed out that only Myrdal could bring it to a proper conclusion with a final report, and that he really needed to return to America to accomplish this. He wrote to Myrdal that "it is a complete mistake when you believe that you have more pressing duties at home." Rather, he said, Myrdal's scholarly abilities could be better put to use in completing the American project now. Sterner also pointed to ideological incentives:

> Perhaps it does not have such a great publicity-value at this time, but there is a chance that it will contribute in a decisive way to a future ideological reconstruction. I do not need to explain further to you, because you grasp surely better than I how a discussion of the Negro question can be recast so that it cuts into the actual basis of the ideological distress which the world suffers under."[7]

Yielding finally to such appeals, Gunnar Myrdal returned to the United States early in 1941. Although Alva remained in Sweden, Gunnar urged her to follow him to America as soon as possible; he seemed unable to focus on his work without her presence. Finally, after great difficulties in managing to make airplane connections through Portugal, Alva joined her husband in October. They then settled at Princeton, where Gunnar— working with his assistants Richard Sterner and Arnold Rose, the latter a young American sociologist—spent a year working on the manuscript of his report. While writing about American race relations, Myrdal was clearly conscious of events in the wider world. As he later said,

> When I was sitting there in Princeton, which was a nice place, I thought about all the youngsters, all my friends in Europe, who were either in prison or killed in war. And here I was sitting and writing my book. It became my war work. And I think this meant much for what the book came to be.[8]

Several other books were being supported by the project, and Myrdal could draw on all these materials by other scholars; but his was supposed to be the centerpiece. He worked very hard for almost a year to bring the manuscript into its final form, then left it in the hands of Rose for the final editing after his return to Sweden. Although a few changes were made in response to criticisms of special reviewers (and the publisher's concern about the length of the work had to be answered), the final result, *An American Dilemma: The Negro Problem and American Democracy,* published in January of 1944, was very much as Myrdal had left it.[9]

The book was impressive in size and scope. It had a text of more than a thousand pages, plus appendices, notes, and an index that extended to page 1403. It dealt with all aspects of race relations in America. It included personal observations of the author as well as more formal social science research. It did not pull any punches in describing the realities of racial discrimination in America. Still, however, it had an optimistic bent, for it pointed toward a future when racial problems would be less severe.

Myrdal's most original contribution in *An American Dilemma* was the context he used for discussing the problems of the American Negro. This context was expressly put in moral terms by countering the democratic ideals of "the American Creed" against the coarse practices of racial discrimination. As he wrote in his introduction, "The American Negro problem is a problem in the heart of the American." He continued:

> Though our study includes economic, social, and political race relations, at bottom our problem is the moral dilemma of the American—the conflict between his moral valuations on various levels of consciousness and generality. The "American Di-lemma," referred to in the title of this book, is the ever-raging conflict between, on the one hand, the valuations preserved on the general plane which we shall call the "American Creed," where the American thinks, talks, and acts under the influence of high national and Christian precepts, and, on the other hand, the valuations on specific planes of individual and group living.[10]

In his conclusions, Myrdal returned to his moral dilemma theme, but he did so with at least a measured degree of hopefulness. He pointed to the increased determination of American blacks to support their cause, to a wide variety of concrete reforms that seemed feasible in the political context of the day (such as abolition of the poll tax or the organization of farm workers into unions), and, above all, to the power of the American Creed in appealing to the American conscience.

An American Dilemma was perhaps the most important book ever written on American race relations. It not only gave a thorough and detailed examination of its subject, but it also set the stage for further debate. Receiving a generally positive response from almost everywhere except the American South, it soon became a central part of the intellectually prevailing views on race relations. It served as both an inspiration for the ensuing Civil Rights movement and as a model of how social science can be made relevant to current problems. Gunnar Myrdal had apparently completed the job for which he had been invited to America.

Onto the World Stage

Alva and Gunnar Myrdal returned to an active role in Swedish society and politics during the final months of World War II. Alva continued her educational leadership and became especially active in Social Democratic postwar planning. Gunnar was again elected to parliament and became the Swedish minister of commerce for two years. Then, in 1947, he received an opportunity for an important position with the United Nations, and he no longer continued in an active role in Swedish politics. A few years later Alva also assumed a leading role on the world stage.

Gunnar's opportunity in 1947 was to head the UN's Economic Commission for Europe (ECE), a post he filled effectively at Geneva for ten years. It was extremely difficult work to undertake with the coming of the Cold War, but Myrdal gained admiration for his economic planning activities in the face of uncertain political events. Not only did his work facilitate reconstruction for Western Europe, but he also sought to lay the foundations for greater East-West trade.

Alva went with Gunnar to Geneva, giving up for the time being most of her other activities. But Gunnar now no longer depended on her for ideas the way he had in past projects, and she soon felt out of place in the more highly ceremonial world of her life in Geneva. Her boredom, however, soon came to an end. In 1949 she accepted a position as head of the UN's Department of Social Welfare, moving to New York's UN headquarters. Soon after that she became chairman of UNESCO's social science section. She traveled widely over the world for her activities in these posts. She also became an important voice for feminism, with *Women's Two Roles: Home and Work* (written with Viola Klein and published in 1956) an important exploration of women's issues.[11]

Alva Myrdal's feminism was central in both her early social activism—seeing gender equality as a key part of all moves toward social reconstruction—and her mature work toward world peace. Feminist values were reinforced by personal experiences throughout her life. As her daughter expressed this theme:

> Children's freedom and that of women and all others from poverty and war and oppression—she could speak out so strongly for these values because she felt them to be indispensable in her own life.[12]

In 1955, Alva Myrdal was appointed to be Sweden's ambassador to India. Two years later her husband gave up his job in Geneva to take on research in South Asian economic development, and once again the Myrdals were together—now mostly in New Delhi. Gunnar's new research project was to study economic development in South Asian countries. This project, supported by the Twentieth Century Fund, was to be as massive a project as had been that of *An American Dilemma*. The results of this work were published in 1968 as *Asian Drama: An Inquiry into the Poverty of Nations*, a three-volume work with more than two thousand pages.[13]

In *Asian Drama*, Gunnar Myrdal surveyed the enormous problems facing poor countries and failed to find any magical formula for their development. He refuted the idea that natural capital accumulation would provide a "take-off point" for development within the world economy. The problems of ingrained poverty and population growth were too severe for that to happen. He also considered foreign aid unlikely to provide sustained development. The nations involved must primarily provide for their own development, and this required careful and long-range planning. Such planning in turn required political stability and an ability to see beyond the immediate pressures. The proposals Myrdal sketched were based on the assumptions that traditional superstitions could give way to rational values, that basically democratic goals would be sought, and that there would need to be strong leadership to promote these goals. All in all, Myrdal was less optimistic in *Asian Drama* than he had been in *An American Dilemma*. But he still saw dedication to democratic values and rational political action as providing the general framework for dealing with fundamental social problems.

Before *Asian Drama* was published, both Gunnar and Alva had returned to Sweden as their primary home base. Gunnar became professor of international economics at Stockholm University, where he founded and directed the Institute for International Economic Studies. Alva again became active in Social Democratic politics and became a member of parliament in 1962. Together the Myrdals established the Stockholm International Peace Research Institute, which soon became one of the world's centers for the study of war and peace issues.

In 1967, Alva Myrdal became a cabinet member of the Swedish government with special responsibilities in the field of disarmament, a field in which she had earlier been given important assignments. She continued in this role for six years. During this time she led Sweden's delegation to the UN Disarmament Conference in Geneva, and Sweden in turn was one of the nations most strongly promoting measures for nuclear disarmament and arms control. Given the state of East-West tensions and the accompanying arms race, this period was not a hospitable time for disarmament proposals. Although everyone gave theoretical support to disarmament, no one—especially not the United States or the Soviet Union—seemed willing to do anything about it. Although she received wide recognition for her efforts, Alva did not feel satisfied with what she was able to accomplish. The final words in her farewell speech in 1973 were: "May I end this last official statement of mine by asking my colleagues: 'When is some action for disarmament to start in earnest?'"[14]

Alva Myrdal's first-hand knowledge and careful analysis of disarmament issues were systematically presented in *The Game of Disarmament*, published in 1976. Here she reviewed all forms of recent disarmament proposals and their Cold War context. Her critique of the arms race mentality of Soviet and American policies was unrelenting, but she also pointed to many possibilities for constructive action in the future. Her survey led her to conclude with an impassioned appeal for public enlightenment while "facing the arms race as the major intellectual and moral dilemma of our time."[15]

Accolades and Accusations

In 1974 the Nobel Prize for Economic Sciences was shared by Gunnar Myrdal and Friedrich von Hayek. Myrdal was not enthusiastic over sharing the prize with Hayek, a conservative free-market proponent whose views on public policy were very different from his own. Nevertheless, they were honored together "for their pioneering work in the theory of money and economic fluctuations and for their penetrating analysis of the interdependence of economic, social and institutional phenomena."[16]

In his special lecture which followed this award, Myrdal dealt with world problems of economic development. He repeated what he had earlier concluded in *Asian Drama* and expressed in his later (1972) book, *The Challenge of World Poverty*. He saw the great gap between the rich and the poor in the world as both a challenge to economic analysis and an appeal to our moral sensitivities.

In 1982, Alva Myrdal was awarded the Nobel Peace Prize, primarily for her work on disarmament issues. The Myrdals thus became the first (and so far, the only) couple to be given Nobel awards for two different areas. After receiving the award Alva repeated the alarm she had sounded in *The Game of Disarmament*. "The actions of those who lead the superpowers," she now said, "are governed by a deep lack of reason and common sense." Still, however, she was unwilling to give up hope for a better future.[17]

During the most active part of her career, Alva Myrdal had moved in circles which were quite independent of those of her husband. At one point she said about their relationship: "Even when duty makes us sail apart, we're still consort battleships." Publicly the picture was that of a happily married couple, though there were frequently tensions that were little noted by others. These included strains between Gunnar and Alva about their expectations for one another, and they also included strains with their children, especially the oldest.[18]

When Jan Myrdal, the first child, was only two, he was left with grandparents in Sweden while his parents spent a year traveling in America. Later he showed many signs of a troubled childhood and at age seventeen made an open break with his family. A very sensitive and widely read writer, Jan eventually turned to recording the memories of his own childhood. In 1980 these began to be published, and the results were not complimentary toward his parents. Gunnar was pictured as an egocentric scholar with little regard for his family and Alva came forth as a cold and calculating woman with powerfully driving ambitions.

In the 1970s, Gunnar and Alva had again found a high level of companionship with each other, often working from opposite sides of their large desk in their common work room. It is ironic that the public picture of their good relationship was ruptured at the very time it had been re-established. Gunnar was enraged to read of his son's descriptions, first published in *Childhood* in 1980 and later continued in other works. Alva was shaken to the roots of her self-confidence. For the rest of their lives they would have to live with their utter rejection at the hands of their oldest child.[19]

Alva Myrdal's deteriorating health (including a brain tumor and aphasia) led the Myrdals to move to a nursing home in 1984. After unsuccessful surgery her condition deteriorated further, and she died on February 1, 1986.

Despite his own weakened condition, Gunnar continued to work on a final project. It was to be a retrospective look at American race relations under the title of *An American Dilemma Revisited*. Since the original publication of *An American Dilemma*, Myrdal had had little to say about its primary subject, though he had touched upon it in a number of lectures and articles. Now he turned his primary attention to it, and the Carnegie Corporation offered what help they could give. But it was too late. Gunnar had difficulty writing or walking because of the advance of Parkinson's disease, and he began to suffer severe lapses of memory. His notes and tapes were not sufficient for what was needed in a new book, which was therefore never completed. His death came on May 17, 1987.

Social Science as Social Engineering

Both Gunnar and Alva Myrdal saw the improvement of human society as the primary task of the social sciences. Gunnar quite explicitly accepted the "social engineering" image for his work, and Alva's efforts were very much in the same direction. They held that it was the job of social science to cultivate increased knowledge about our social arrangements, with the end that these arrangements might be changed to improve the lives of ordinary people.

Values are central in all the processes of social research. As Gunnar Myrdal has expressed this point,

> There can be no such thing as disinterested research. Valuations enter into social research not only when drawing policy conclusions but already when searching for facts and when establishing the relationship between facts.

There are no completely objective facts, in this view. Facts have meaning in relation to the questions asked, and the questions asked always come out of one's assumptions about society.[20]

But this does not mean that everything is subjective, depending on an individual researcher's arbitrary point of view. Points of view themselves can be validated as social values are laid bare and research questions are posed. The search for facts can also be extremely difficult and challenging, especially when they are arranged to show their policy implications. For instance, Gunnar Myrdal did not just passively collect facts about American race relations. He sought them in a research framework that would grow out of the values inherent in American society. Once the outlines of the "American Creed" were identified, the facts of racial discrimination began to point toward needed changes in social policies. The disarmament issue provided a similar challenge for Alva Myrdal. She held that the values of a more peaceful world must be kept ever in mind as we view the nuclear arsenals and the Cold War policies of the superpowers.

Once the policy implications of a particular area of social research become clear, the Myrdals held that it is the responsibility of the social scientist to persuade his or her colleagues—by presenting the facts and their implications—about the wisdom of certain social policies. As those social scientists in a given field come to see the same implications, the task then becomes that of educating the general public. The social scientist's job is not finished with a list of proposed policies; there is also the responsibility for seeing that these enter fairly into the public debate.

Gunnar and Alva Myrdal did their best to do painstaking research that was most relevant to great social issues—issues such as race, poverty, and war. But their work did not end with the tabulation of facts. It extended on into how we might most effectively bring about changes in social attitudes and institutions based on our best knowledge. The general betterment of society was always their ultimate objective.

There is in all this an ultimate faith in the value of human reason for bringing about intelligent social change. This was clearly expressed in the final paragraph in *An American Dilemma*, where Gunnar Myrdal wrote,

> To find the practical formulas for this never-ending reconstruction of society is the supreme task of social science. The world catastrophe places tremendous difficulties in our way and may shake our confidence to the depths. Yet we have today in social science a greater trust in the improvability of man and society than we have ever had since the Enlightenment.[21]

10

C. Wright Mills:
The Social Scientist as Rebel

Out of Texas

In his book *White Collar*, C. Wright Mills characterizes the family life of the "midget entrepreneur" (or "lumpen-bourgeoisie") class with the following words:

> The family circle is closed in and often withdrawn into itself, thus encouraging strong intimacies and close-up hatreds. The children of such families are often the objects upon which parental frustrations are projected. They are subjected alternatively to overindulgence, which springs from close parental competition for their affection, and to strong discipline, which is based on the parents' urge to 'make the child amount to something.' In the meantime continual deprivations are justified in terms of the future success of the children, who must give up things now, but who, by doing so, may legitimately claim the rewards of great deference and gratification in the future.[1]

The above passage refers to the niche in society in which Charles Wright Mills was born in Waco, Texas, on August 28, 1916. His father was an insurance agent, and the family moved frequently. His parents were of mixed Irish and English stock. Due mainly to the influence of his mother, Mills was raised as a Roman Catholic, though he ceased to be a practicing member of that faith during adolescence. Still, in the several Texas towns where Mills spent his boyhood, his Catholicism must have set him off from the more numerous Baptists and other Protestants.

His mother commented on her son's "unbeatable will." Apparently he would stand up to his parents, teachers and other children and refuse to yield whenever he felt he was right. For example, when he was only seven, his family moved to a new area and he was to be put back a year in school. Young Charlie then simply refused to attend school under these terms, and his parents finally arranged with the principal that he be placed in the class which he demanded.[2]

By and large Mills looked back at his childhood as lonely years. In fact, a certain loneliness seemed to characterize much of his career. Late in his life he was to comment that "I have never known what others call 'fraternity' with any group...neither academic nor political." Nevertheless, he had faith in his own abilities, which were early nurtured in a technical direction. While attending high school in Dallas, he took no social studies work other than the civics and history requirements. Instead, he enrolled in the courses that fit his plan for a career in engineering.

After graduating from high school in 1934, he enrolled in the Texas Agricultural and Mechanical College. This was intended, in his father's view, "to make a man of him." The result, however, did not go according to this plan, and he was later to look back at his friendless year at Texas A & M as among his most miserable experiences.[3]

Mills then transferred to the University of Texas at Austin, which he found to be a much more congenial environment. He actually made a few close friends there, and found intellectual excitement in his studies in sociology, economics, and philosophy. Sociology became his declared field, though philosophical issues seemed to attract his greatest attention. His interest was especially involved in the study of pragmatic philosophers such as John Dewey and George H. Mead. In 1939, he graduated with both baccalaureate and master's degrees received the same day (his undergraduate degree was delayed by his failure to meet certain undergraduate requirements in a timely manner). His master's thesis, "Reflection, Behavior and Culture," showed his early interest in pragmatic philosophy and the sociology of knowledge.

During his junior year at Texas, Mills married Dorothy Smith, a social activist with significant writing and social skills. She seemed to have complemented well some of her young husband's limitations. Soon they had a daughter. However, the marriage was filled with tension and lasted only a few years.

After Texas, Mills pursued the doctorate at the University of Wisconsin. He first sought an assistantship in philosophy there, but when he was not successful in this he shifted to sociology. He soon became known as an outstanding sociology student. He came with articles already accepted by significant sociology journals, and with very good references from Texas. For example, the philosopher and economist Clarence Ayres saw him as "tremendously eager and incredibly energetic." Another of his Texas teachers had given him a more guarded recommendation, which said in part:

> Under the proper influences, he might develop into an unusually able student. In the past he has at time been somewhat temperamental, but he seems to be outgrowing that condition. His main source of trouble was formerly a certain arrogance that

aroused hostility among the persons he criticized. I think he has overcome most, if not all, of this at the present time. He may still need a bit of discipline, but I think he might repay the effort.

It is not clear that anyone at Wisconsin was successful in imposing such a "bit of discipline" upon Mills in his two years there. Nevertheless, he did profit from his studies, which continued to focus more on his own interests than on degree requirements.[4]

Mills became especially close to one of the young faculty members at Wisconsin, Hans Gerth. They found many interests in common and began a collaboration that was to bear fruit in two books later—*From Max Weber*, a collection of Weber's essays that Gerth translated and that Mills worked with him in editing, was published in 1946; and *Character and Social Structure*, by Gerth and Mills, finally appeared in 1953.[5]

Mills' relationships were decidedly cool to other sociologists at Wisconsin, including John Gillin, the department chairman. He saw Gillin's work as typical of those sociologists who write about social problems. They, he said in an article ("The Professional Ideology of Social Pathologists," published shortly after he left Wisconsin), provide "a reformism dealing with masses of detail" but offer "no bases for points of entry for larger social action in a structureless flux." His relation to his advisor Howard Becker seemed even more strained. He saw this relationship as both a clash of politics (he considered Becker to be a reactionary) and of personalities. Mills refused to change some of the things in his dissertation as Becker directed. He declined to make other changes demanded by his committee. The question was then evident: what were they then to do about this obviously brilliant but unruly student? The committee never formally approved Mills' final product (titled "A Sociological Account of Pragmatism") but they did let the dissertation stand and allowed Mills to claim his Wisconsin Ph.D. in 1942.[6]

Perceiving Patterns of Power

Mills found his first faculty position at the University of Maryland. He never saw this institution as a final destination for his career; however, it was close to Washington D.C., where so much was going on during those years of 1941-45. His activities during this period were more in Washington than at Maryland's College Park campus, the site of his formal teaching duties.

Mills' Maryland years coincided with those of America's involvement in World War II. Mills was basically opposed to this war. While no admirer of Nazi Germany, he felt that the war would only move American society toward its own form of totalitarianism. He considered briefly going to prison if drafted, but he was relieved to find himself rejected for military service on the basis of his hypertension.

Mills had not previously been a political activist. As he wrote to Hans Gerth early in 1942, "I am a political youngster. I never paid any attention to political affairs until last year, or better, until this year in Washington." But Mills soon became heavily involved in political discussions and writing. He was among those who saw capitalism as the chief problem for the development of a democratic society in America. In particular, it was the alliance between government and the monopoly capitalists that was the basis of the threat to a free society. This was not a doctrinaire Marxism (only later did Mills become a serious student of Marx), but the way Mills naturally saw the world as he became part of the momentous events of the early 1940s. He freely expressed his emerging political views in such publications as the *New Leader, New Republic*, and *Partisan Review*.[7]

In the fall of 1944, Mills let it be known to selected individuals that he was not committed to staying on at Maryland indefinitely. Robert K. Merton, then at Columbia University, was among those to whom he wrote, and Merton helped to arrange an appointment at Columbia. Although there were no regular faculty positions then available, Columbia's Bureau of Applied Social Research, headed by Paul Lazarsfeld, offered another possibility. In 1945, Mills accepted an appointment in that social research organization, and this led to a regular faculty position the following year.

His applied social research work at Columbia had for Mills both positive and negative aspects. One clearly positive feature was that it brought him to New York, where he had already formed many personal associations and previously established a summer home in Greenwich Village. Also, it gave him an association with a highly prestigious university. Not the least of the positive elements was his acquaintance with Ruth Harper, a statistician at the bureau. With his first marriage ended, he was soon to become married to Ms. Harper.

But Mills also had problems with his bureau appointment. He was not used to busying himself with the details of social research, and the kinds of applied research in which he found himself involved seemed out of place with the image of a big-picture intellectual he had established for himself. He learned more about empirical research, but in doing so the patience of those with whom he worked was sometimes stretched thin.

He had a tendency to seek ideological angles in his bureau projects, which did not fit the neutral style of applied research that Lazarsfeld had developed.

Mills also had problems with project administration. For example, one of the projects for which he had responsibility, a study of local leadership in Decatur, Illinois, had nearly exhausted its budget while still in its data gathering phase. This was not acceptable, and Lazarsfeld was forced to take over the project himself, juggling department research funds to allow its completion. As a replacement assignment Mills was given leadership for a study of Puerto Rican immigrants in New York. This led to one of his early books, *The Puerto Rican Journey*, published in 1950. In the end, both the Decatur and Puerto Rican projects were successfully completed, but not without a variety of administrative difficulties.[8]

Mills never fit easily with his sociological colleagues at Columbia. By mutual consent he soon ended his association with the bureau, but he still remained aloof from most other departmental activities. His time was mostly devoted to teaching undergraduate classes and pursuing his own projects. In that way he could avoid involving himself in what he saw as the trivia of academic life.

The New Men of Power, published in 1948, was Mills' first book. This brought together the skills that he had developed for social research with his ideological criticism of American social structure. At first glance, this was simply another sociological study of a particular group—500 leaders of organized labor in the United States—with the usual supply of statistical tables and analysis. But his critical mind and power with words led Mills to use this work as part of a much broader analysis of social stratification in America. This would be continued with his books on the American class system: *White Collar* (published in 1951) and *The Power Elite* (appearing in 1956).[9]

The leaders of labor—in a sense, the power elite of the working class— appeared in *The New Men of Power* to have only a very limited sense of their ability to bring about change in American society. Much more were they the functionaries of the established framework of political and economic power. This disappointed Mills, for in his radical vision labor leaders should, in tandem with left-wing intellectuals (such as Mills), be leading the way to create a more egalitarian society. Instead, he found them generally supporting an ineffective liberalism. "The liberals," he complained, "want changes, but the means they would use and the practicality they espouse are short-run and small-scale." This was not the radical vision Mills would have preferred.[10]

Even less did Mills find leadership for social change among the American middle classes. *White Collar* describes the new middle classes of managers, professionals, office workers, and sales personnel as entering quietly into a world which was not of their own making, and with little insight about what they might do to improve their ways of life. This somber view is well captured in the final paragraph of the book, in which Mills gives the following picture of the political views of the new middle classes:

> Since they have no public position, their private positions as individuals determine in what direction each of them goes; but, as individuals, they do not know where to go. So now they waver. They hesitate, confused and vacillating in their opinions, unfocused and discontinuous in their actions. They are worried and distrustful but, like so many others, they have no targets on which to focus their worry and distrust. They may be politically irritable, but they have no political passion.[11]

If Mills describes the middle classes in *White Collar* as largely nonpolitical, the same cannot be said about those he saw as residing at the top of the American social structure. In *The Power Elite* Mills examines the patterns of national power observed in the United States over a period of a hundred years, and he concludes that power has become increasingly concentrated in the heads of large bureaucratic organizations. The government, large private corporations, and, increasingly, the military provide the main sources of power in America, and those at the top of organizations in these areas have more and more become the managers of their society. The general public is only vaguely aware of the power of its small group of leaders, for the display of power is inhibited by the rhetoric of democracy. Increasingly, however, the lives of ordinary men and women are constrained by the decisions made by those in charge of our powerful bureaucracies.[12]

His three books on social stratification provided Mills with a way of combining his skills as a social analyst with those of a social prophet. Although some sociologists were disappointed by his rather unsystematic methods of data analysis, he did provide a fresh look at the frameworks of power in American society. His view was strongly political, with social power no longer viewed as mainly an extension of economic forces. Also, he gave a prophetic stance to his analysis. He was not enamored by the trends he observed. American society, he suggested, could be other than it was. Without directly saying so, Mills suggested that a more democratic vision could be realized by the American people if they would only listen to what socially conscious intellectuals (such as Mills himself) had to say about their political choices.

The Sociological Imagination and Beyond

Mills saw himself within what he called "the classic tradition" of sociological work. This tradition included such figures as Karl Marx, Herbert Spencer, Vilfredo Pareto, Émile Durkheim, and Max Weber. In his *Images of Man*, Mills viewed those of this tradition not so much in terms of their particular theories but rather in terms of the questions they raised about the nature of human society.

> These questions are generally of wide scope: they concern total societies, their transformations, and the varieties of individual men and women that inhabit them. The answers given by classic sociologists provide conceptions about society, about history and about biography, and in their work these three are usually linked closely together. The structure of society and the mechanics of history are seen within the same perspective, and within this perspective changes in human nature are also defined.[13]

In his undergraduate years at Texas, Mills insisted on raising general questions about the nature of man and society. He found important answers in such authors as Thorstein Veblen, George Herbert Mead, and Karl Mannheim. In his graduate work at Wisconsin, his contacts with Hans Gerth led to a special role for Max Weber. He joined Gerth in editing a volume of Weber's writings and preparing a book on social psychology. The latter, when finally published in 1953 as *Character and Social Structure* drew especially upon Freud, Marx, Mead, and Weber for insights into the linkage between persons and their social institutions. In his great works on stratification (especially in *White Collar* and *The Power Elite*) Mills saw himself as continuing this "classic tradition." However, it is in *The Sociological Imagination* that Mills most clearly states how he sees his work rooted in this tradition—and different from so much of what other social scientists were doing.[14]

"It is my aim in this book to define the meaning of the social sciences for the cultural tasks of our time." Mills uses these words to summarize his efforts in writing *The Sociological Imagination*. Note that he here talks of the social sciences and not just sociology. The quality of imagination he calls "sociological" is not limited to one discipline, but belongs to all the social sciences. However, he seems to feel that sociologists have a special responsibility for rediscovering the rich imagination of their classic tradition—if for no other reason than that they seem so willing to forget it in favor of their contemporary styles of "grand theory" and "abstracted empiricism."[15]

Note also the breadth of purpose Mills sees in "the cultural tasks of our times." This is not a simple discussion of the social sciences for professionals in the field. Mills' reach extends much further. He sought to write about the general intellectual malaise of our age, and how it may be best addressed.

"Nowadays," Mills begins his book, "men often feel that their private lives are a series of traps." They feel that they can do little by themselves to overcome their private troubles. They are largely correct in this, Mills feels, for they fail to see their own troubles rooted in the larger sweep of history. What they need is a larger perspective into which they may place their smaller worlds. "Neither the life of an individual nor the history of a society can be understood without understanding both," says Mills, and it is his purpose to encompass both within what he calls "the sociological imagination."[16]

"The sociological imagination enables us to grasp history and biography and the relations between the two within society. That is its task and its promise." So says Mills. To fulfill the demands of such an imagination we must "range from the most impersonal and remote transformations to the most intimate features of the human self—and to see the relations between the two." With the aid of such a view "men can now hope to grasp what is going on in the world, and to understand what is happening in themselves as minute points of the intersections of biography and history within society."[17]

It is quite clear that Mills seeks to promote enlightenment for persons in general, not just for those who call themselves social scientists. It is, he believes, one of the great tasks of social science to provide the understanding that will make such a result possible. This requires us to show how personal troubles of individuals are related to the public issues of their social structures. Let us take note of one of the examples that Mills cites here:

> Consider war. The personal problem of war, when it occurs, may be how to survive it or how to die in it with honor; how to make money out of it; how to climb into the higher safety of the military apparatus; or how to contribute to the war's termination. In short, according to one's values, to find a set of milieux and within it to survive the war or make one's death in it meaningful. But the structural issues of war have to do with its causes; with what types of men it throws up into command; with its effects upon economic and political, family and religious institutions, with the unorganized irresponsibility of a world of nation-states.

In order to accomplish the promise of the sociological imagination, then, we must be very much aware of the varieties of social structure and how social structural issues are related to the troubles experienced by individuals within them. And we must seek to make this knowledge widely available—not just as research reports in social science journals.[18]

Such is the vision Mills sets forth in the opening pages of *The Socio-logical Imagination*. After presenting this framework in his first chapter, he spends the next five (over half of the book) pointing to what is wrong with the contemporary world of social science. He seems particularly eager to point to the failings of sociologists with their pretensions at "grand theory" and their meaningless ventures in "abstracted empiri-cism." He fulminates at the increasingly bureaucratic organization of social science research and condemns the tendencies of its practitioners to serve the interests of the highest bidder. Against all this he sets an agenda inspired by the true "sociological imagination." Those following this banner would use their research (usually quite broad-based) to show how private troubles are related to public issues, to clarify those public issues in terms of the fundamental interests of people involved, and to provide intellectual guidance for the great tasks of social change. Mills sums up his plea with the following words:

> What I am suggesting is that by addressing ourselves to issues and to troubles, and formulating them as problems of social science, we stand the best chance, I believe the only chance, to make reason democratically relevant to human affairs in a free society, and so realize the classic values that underlie the promise of our studies.[19]

For his work in *The Sociological Imagination*, Mills received mixed reviews. Most academic social scientists were highly critical, for he had seemed so eager to denigrate leading forms of contemporary theory and research. In periodicals of wider circulation his criticisms of pompous theory and the minutia of research found a stronger appeal. Among his colleagues at Columbia University was the feeling that Mills had unfairly turned against the respectable scientific activities they had worked so hard to nourish. Paul Lazarsfeld felt most personally attacked, but oth-ers also felt outraged. But this little mattered to Mills. He had become a full professor there in 1956, and he now felt free to define his intel-lectual independence however he pleased. Although he never ended his association with Columbia, he moved more and more in other circles, and in his last years he found his identify more as a citizen of the world than as an American sociologist.

Mills did not visit Europe before 1956, when he was a Fulbright lecturer at the University of Copenhagen. Thereafter he traveled widely in Europe, including a notable visit to the Soviet Union in 1960, and in Latin America (especially in Mexico and Cuba). In late 1961, just a few months before his death, he was thinking of taking up permanent residence in England.

Separated from his second wife after ten years of marriage, Mills married again in 1959 to a New York artist, Yaroslava Surmach. The following year they had a son, making Mills a father of one child in each of his three marriages. Mills and Yara, as he called his new wife, built a new home outside New York City, but they also felt free to travel abroad.

During the final years of his life, Mills' writings became less analytical and more strident—and his audience extended more and more widely. His success with *White Collar* and *The Power Elite* had made him a celebrity, and now he built on this with works written even more directly for a popular audience. He became a hero to many who shared his causes, though others felt that his work increasingly lacked analytical balance. Those in the peace movement made wide use of *The Causes of World War III*, which pictured the Soviet and American empires as pushing blindly toward a catastrophe for the whole world. Other critics of American foreign policy found much to acclaim in *Listen, Yankee!*, in which he seemed to identify strongly with Castro's Cuban Revolution. Such work showed the involvement of Mills in world political issues, but it was a step away from the careful analysis of his earlier sociological works.[20]

His sympathies toward the Cuban revolution were especially controversial. His views, published in *Harper's Magazine* as well as in book form, brought careful scrutiny from the F.B.I. His views on Cuba led to preparations for a scheduled debate on national television at the end of 1960; however, the day before the debate was to occur, Mills suffered a major heart attack. Health problems continued for the rest of his life, but he remained professionally active until another major heart attack brought death on March 20, 1962. Most of the last year of his life was spent with his new family in Western Europe and the Soviet Union, but he had returned to his home in the United States shortly before his death.

Published just after his death was *The Marxists*, a serious study of the varieties of Marxism. Here Mills showed himself to be sympathetic to the fundamental thinking of Karl Marx but critical of the forms that Marxism had created for the twentieth century.[21]

When Mills died he had rather ambitious plans for future work. These included a series of studies in comparative sociology, describing social structures in all parts of the world and projected to extend through at least six volumes. Had he lived, this project might well have become his most important contribution to sociological analysis.

The Social Scientist as Rebel

It is difficult to sum up the central contribution of C. Wright Mills to social science, and even more difficult to capture his defining essence as a human being.

As a social scientist he could be coolly analytic, but also sometimes he showed extreme passion for a cause. As a man he showed features that often seemed in sharp contradiction to each other. For example, he ridiculed the way others devoted themselves to their work, but he was relentless in the way he drove himself in his own work. He was also a heavy-drinking man who enjoyed driving around Manhattan Island on his motorcycle—as relentless with his efforts in play as in work.

Irving Louis Horowitz, at the end of what is probably the most thorough study of the life and work of Mills, has described some of his personal contradictions:

> He was a pragmatic anarchist, and no less a conservative radical. He was against the Second World War but never surrendered his claims on the usefulness of violence. He had a touching rural town hall approach to settling political disputes, and yet advocated cosmopolitan life-styles. He was for rugged individualism and yet opposed a social system fostering and advocating such an ideology. He never so much as voted, yet he offered political advice to anyone who would listen. He opposed the civil culture as profoundly antipolitical, yet he rejected political participation because it destroyed the civic culture.[22]

The final image Horowitz presents for Mills is that of "an American utopian." His thought—though similar in some senses with that of classic European sociologists such as Marx, Weber, and Durkheim—showed strongly the imprint of American popular democracy. And despite the cynical manner in which he frequently treated the expressed idealism of others, Mills had his own central ideals of truth and freedom. He always sought the truth, however elusive it might be, and he never gave up on his search for what might be achieved in a more rational society.

Mills could never fit easily into his personal or professional circles. He always appeared to be seeking something other than what he was or had. But in this seeking he provided a lens through which American society could be seen more clearly. Few other social scientists could write with the lucid insight which Mills provided.

"The creative rebel" is how we might best characterize C. Wright Mills and his work as a social scientist.

11

Daniel Patrick Moynihan: The Social Scientist as Politician

From the Sidewalks of New York

When it endorsed the campaign of Daniel Patrick Moynihan to run for the U.S. Senate in 1976, the *New York Times* called him, among other things, "that rambunctious child of the sidewalks of New York." This endorsement was not without controversy (to accomplish it the publisher overrode the judgment of the editorial page editor), and controversy seems to have been part of the career of Moynihan at nearly every stage. But can there be any doubt that his life was forever shaped by growing up in New York City?[1]

Moynihan was indeed a product of New York, but he had other roots as well. His father, John, who usually found employment as a journalist, grew up in a comfortable middle-class home in eastern Indiana, and his mother, Margaret, was the daughter of a successful lawyer in southern Indiana. Shortly after their marriage in 1925, they moved to Tulsa, Oklahoma, where John worked for the *Tulsa Tribune*. It was in Tulsa that their first child was born on March 16, 1927. Thus began the life of Daniel Patrick Moynihan.

A few months later, the family moved to New York, where John got a job as an advertising copywriter. They lived briefly in Greenwich Village, then in suburban communities in New Jersey and Long Island. By 1937 there were two more children—then, suddenly, they were without a father. John increasingly spent his time with drinking and gambling friends, then simply left home. "Marriage broke up," Moynihan later summed up his world at that point, "and down we went."[2]

Devastated by this sudden change in family fortunes, the mother sought whatever jobs she could find to support the family, which lived in a series of low-rent apartments in Manhattan. The boys—Pat and his younger brother Mike—brought in money by shining shoes at Times Square and in Central Park. For a few years Margaret remarried—which brought the children temporarily into a more comfortable home, though with a despised stepfather. Living in Westchester County until the mother's second marriage ended in 1941, the Moynihan children attended a more upscale school where Pat found it difficult to fit in easily. With America's entry into the war, however, jobs became more available, and Margaret Moynihan soon found herself as chief nurse in a war production plant and able to afford a large apartment in Queens. Young Pat no longer was limited to shining shoes to help support his family; he could make more money selling newspapers and working as a stock boy in Gimbels department store or as a stevedore on the New York piers.

Pat did well in school. Returning to Manhattan from Westchester in 1941, he enrolled in Benjamin Franklin High School in East Harlem. Two years later he graduated as valedictorian, class secretary, and a member of the honor society. That summer, while working the piers, he saw an announcement of an entrance examination for the City College of New York. He decided to follow up on this possibility, and soon found himself in college, even while continuing to work on the waterfront.

The following year Pat entered an officer training program of the U. S. Navy. His college work continued, but now under the auspices of the Navy. He first went to Middlebury College in Vermont, then continued in the ROTC program at Tufts University, where he received his A.B. degree in naval science. Although World War II was over by this time, he began his active duty on the *USS Quirinus*, where he served as a communications officer. In 1947 he began graduate studies at Tufts, which he continued even while he was involved in other activities—such as serving as a lumberjack in Montana and helping his mother run a bar in the Hell's Kitchen area of New York City.

In 1950 he was given a Fulbright award to study at the London School of Economics. Although originally planning his studies in England to be for only nine months, he was able to extend his time there for two more years, providing both academic studies in the social sciences and familiarity with the details of British political life.

Returning to New York in 1953, Pat spent a year employed as director of public relations for the International Rescue Committee, a voluntary organization working with refugees. He also entered heartily into the Democratic politics of New York, working first with Robert Wagner's successful campaign for mayor and then, in 1954, on the campaign that brought Averell Harriman into the governor's office. Associated in this campaign with the man who became the governor's executive secretary, Moynihan was also invited to Albany to serve with the Harriman administration. He left his IRC position to become for the governor a man whose talents were used in any way most needed—entertaining visitors, writing reports, and helping to supervise whatever went on in the governor's office.

While Pat Moynihan was working with a refugee agency, a young woman named Elizabeth Brennan was also in New York, working for the Health Information Foundation. She also became heavily involved in Harriman's 1954 campaign, and as a result was invited to be part of Governor Harriman's staff in Albany, with the primary duty of taking care of his personal correspondence. This soon brought her into close contact with Pat, who almost immediately was proposing marriage. Pat and Liz were married in 1955. Liz continued only briefly with full-time work, for the three Moynihan children had all been born by the end of 1960. By then, however, Harriman had lost his reelection bid to Nelson Rockefeller, and Pat Moynihan had begun his first university job at Syracuse.

The Professor

Pat Moynihan always did well in school. He graduated from high school first in his class. His B.A. from Tufts was given *cum laude* in 1948, and his M.A. followed the next year at the Fletcher School of Law and Diplomacy. The fact that he was soon on the way to the London School of Economics with a Fulbright grant speaks well of the academic promise of the young man. But his academic learning seemed always secondary to what he learned about urban life by living and working in New York City. About the impact of his London studies, he later recalled: "I did know Karl Popper, went to his lectures, having read *The Open Society and Its Enemies* while at Fletcher. But nothing and no one at LSE ever disposed me to be anything but a New York Democrat who had some friends who worked on the docks and drank beer after work."[3]

Moynihan's own Ph.D. did not seem his highest priority during the years he worked on it. The project that was to become his dissertation was begun during his London years, but it appeared to take a back seat to his activities in the New York governor's office. His subject of study was the early history of the International Labor Organization, which then seemed further from his interests than the in-fighting among New York Democrats.

When Harriman lost his bid for reelection, his papers were given to the Maxwell School of Citizenship and Public Affairs at Syracuse University, and Moynihan was assigned there to the job of writing a history of the Harriman administration. This first faculty appointment for Moynihan—heavily geared to political research—produced no scholarly publications. His history of the Harriman administration never went beyond a first draft, mainly because the ex-governor was not happy with what Moynihan had written (not flattering enough, apparently, Moynihan later decided). But during his two years at Syracuse, Moynihan did finish his doctoral work. He had almost thrown away his dissertation notes during one of the moves he made with his family, but now he found special encouragement from his dean to finish the project. He was officially awarded the degree from the Fletcher School at Tufts in 1961.

Moynihan's early publications showed him to be an active intellectual with a wide variety of interests, but they were not heavily scholarly. He contributed to such journals as *The Reporter*, *Commentary*, and *Commonweal*. His first article was on traffic safety, a subject he had been involved with for Governor Harriman. He brought a new perspective to this subject, viewing traffic accidents more like medical epidemics than as the results of judgment or bad luck of individuals. He was later to apply this epidemiological approach to fruitful analyses of drug use and violent crime.[4]

Political commentary was also a natural area for Moynihan's early writing. The role of state government and Democratic Party politics were among the subjects he treated. However, it was the subject of ethnicity that first brought him wide recognition among social scientists. Nathan Glazer, a sociologist with previous work on American character and author of *The Social Basis of American Communism,* had spent several years in developing a project on ethnicity in New York City. Starting with a small grant from the New York *Post*, Glazer planned to have different authors discuss the main ethnic groups. He early had Moynihan in mind for the Irish. As the project evolved, it became the joint work of Glazer and Moynihan. It was finally published in 1963 as a book, *Beyond the Melting Pot*, by the Joint Center for Urban Studies at Harvard and the Massachusetts Institute of Technology.[5]

At a time when many social scientists were viewing ethnicity as a legacy from the past but a generally declining force for the present, Glazer and Moynihan sought to treat it as a central feature of modern society—at least so far as New York City was concerned. "The notion that the intense and unprecedented mixture of ethnic and religious groups in American life was soon to blend into a homogeneous end product has outlived its usefulness, and also its credibility," they stated in their preface, and the rest of the book documents the changing face but persisting patterns of major ethnic groups in New York. American events of the next few years seemed to vindicate the point of view of the authors, and subsequent worldwide explosions of ethnicity have further demonstrated the importance of ethnic identity in the modern world.

By the time *Beyond the Melting Pot* was published, Moynihan was back in government work, where ethnicity was a very practical problem for him. This soon became widely recognized when "The Moynihan Report" was circulated in 1965. We will later describe this document, but for now it may simply serve to illustrate how closely tied together were Moynihan's concerns as a social scientist with those of his government service.

After five years with the federal government, Moynihan again returned to an academic setting, as a fellow in the Center for Advanced Studies at Wesleyan University. He was then offered the position of director for the Joint Center for Urban Studies at MIT and Harvard in 1966. He continued to teach at Harvard—first as professor of education and urban politics, and then as professor of government—until 1977. During some of this time he was on leave for further government service, for he closely combined his public and academic careers. Most of his later books, such as those he edited on urban affairs and poverty, grew out of both his academic scholarship and his wide experience in government.[6]

Even while involved in government programs, Moynihan had the critical eye of the social scientist. And he took very seriously his commitments as a professor. For example, as all his friends were celebrating his initial election to the U.S. Senate from New York late on election night in 1976, he excused himself early from the festivities. He returned to Harvard, where the next morning he met his class in "Social Science and Social Policy" as he had regularly done throughout his campaign.

Pursuing New Frontiers

Moynihan naturally supported John Kennedy in the 1960 election, though his duties at Syracuse limited his political activities. His wife was more active in this campaign than he, though he did help Governor Harriman write a brief speech to second Kennedy's nomination when the Democratic convention reached its point of decision. Both Pat and Liz Moynihan hoped they could be part of the new administration in some way, and their feelers were soon out for jobs in several areas. Nothing seemed promising until a longtime friend, Sandy Vanocur, then a reporter with NBC, pointed out that Arthur Goldberg was seeking professional staff members in his Department of Labor. Pat was soon identified as a special assistant to the secretary of labor, and the Moynihans prepared to move to Washington.

Moynihan was already at work at Labor when a hitch developed over the appointment. The Federal Bureau of Investigation had raised some questions about his suitability for government employment. Agents came to interview him in the Department of Labor and strongly suggested that there were serious issues about Moynihan's record. He had just published an article in *The Reporter* which was highly critical of FBI policies and of J. Edgar Hoover, its director; this fact was probably not unrelated to the special investigation of Moynihan. Secretary Goldberg did not yield to the pressure, though he did call in his new special assistant to suggest that it might be helpful for Pat to go to J. Edgar Hoover to explain personally his side of the story. This Moynihan sought to do, but the Director declined to meet with him. FBI records indicate that Hoover was given a memo in advance of the proposed interview which concluded:

> Moynihan is an egghead that talks in circles and constantly contradicts himself. He shifts about constantly in his chair and will not look you in the eye. He would be the first so-called "liberal" that would scream if the FBI overstepped its jurisdiction. He is obviously a phony intellectual that one minute will back down and the next minute strike while our back is turned. I think we made numerous points in our interview with him, however, this man is so much up on "cloud nine" it is doubtful that his ego will allow logical interpretation of remarks made to other people.

To this Hoover penned the response: "I am not going to see this skunk." The appointment was then allowed to be concluded without further objection from the FBI.[7]

Comfortable socially, a man with easy ideas, an excellent writer, and a hard worker, Moynihan soon made significant contributions to the Kennedy administration. One of his first tasks was in an area that normally would not be expected to go with his official position. He turned a job no one else seemed to want—representing Labor in an Ad Hoc Committee on Federal Office Space—into a significant contribution for urban planning. Accepting the job of writing the committee's report, Moynihan included in it a clear statement of "Guiding Principles for Federal Architecture." He argued persuasively that the most modern forms of artistic design could be used to embody the great traditions of American government when applied thoughtfully and without trying to make any particular pattern into an official style. The report also dealt with the physical decay at the heart of official Washington—in particular, along Pennsylvania Avenue between the Capitol and the White House. This attracted the personal attention of the president, who was planning to share this part of the report with congressional leaders when his untimely death occurred in November of 1963. The Pennsylvania Avenue project was given new life by President Johnson in response to the expressed wishes of Jacqueline Kennedy. Decades later, when Moynihan was in the Senate, the main goals of the project were finally achieved.

One morning in the summer of 1963, Moynihan found an item in the *Washington Post* that started him thinking. The Selective Service System was rejecting almost half of the young men it examined for the military draft. This, Moynihan felt, should be considered a major problem, and he convinced the secretary of labor (by then Willard Wirtz, after Goldberg's appointment to the Supreme Court) to arrange for a presidential task force on this problem. Moynihan became secretary when the group was appointed, and as such he wrote its report. This report, titled "One Third of a Nation," was given to President Johnson on January 1, 1964. The president was then in the middle of planning a war on poverty, and the statistics and tables in this brief report helped to document his concern. The nation was not preparing many young Americans for the jobs being created—and not just in the military services. This was just another piece of evidence to support the idea that bold new measures were required to confront the poverty remaining in America.

Moynihan, now assistant secretary of labor for planning and research, was brought onto the central stage for plotting the war on poverty. He was among the key figures helping to formulate what so quickly was to become the Economic Opportunity Act of 1964. Administration planners of this legislation were not united in the way they wished to assault the problem of poverty. Some of the social science experts brought into the discussion emphasized "community action" as a key means of dealing with juvenile delinquency. They seemed to assume that a decentralized system, developed within the context of the local community and led by social work professionals, would have the greatest impact in changing the lives of America's poor. Moynihan was among those who saw the problem in other terms. The problem of the poor, he insisted, is primarily a lack of money. He felt that to play with their lives through special programs would be of little benefit unless they were provided the means for fuller employment or better work incomes.[8]

What was finally included in the proposed (and enacted) legislation was a compromise between the positions of the various administration groups. There was a community action program component, which Moynihan had opposed, but he had only minor reservations about the rest of Johnson's anti-poverty program as it came to be established and administered by Sargent Shriver, brother-in-law of the late President Kennedy.

By the end of 1964, Moynihan and two of his staff members had begun a research paper which would be titled "The Negro Family: The Case for National Action," though most frequently referred to as simply "The Moynihan Report." No one had specifically asked for this paper—it came at Moynihan's own initiative. But it appeared to be most timely and almost immediately became the focus of policy discussions at the highest level. It brought Daniel P. Moynihan's name into the center of controversy more than any other thing he ever did.[9]

Moynihan felt that the way the anti-poverty program had been crafted, a key issue had been brushed aside—that of race. Also, he felt that the Civil Rights Act of 1964 had neglected to address some of the social factors most critical for the future of American race relations. In any event, he believed that there were special problems in black communities which were making progress difficult for them, and at the heart of these difficulties was the matter of family structure.

Many social scientists before Moynihan had pointed out that blacks and whites in America differed in family patterns, but none had raised this issue so directly into the deliberations of national public policy. Also, although the figures and tables of the Moynihan Report tended to document what many American social scientists already knew, there were a few new points. By using the latest data available to the federal government, Moynihan was able to show that some of the historic patterns were changing in ways which were bound to add to the problems of American race relations. For example, the correlations between black unemployment and AFDC (public aid to dependent children) to black families no longer showed trend lines in common. It appeared that there was an emerging disconnect between economic aid and family stability. This suggested that simply increasing aid programs might not be effective in bringing lasting improvements for black communities.

Most of the seventy-eight pages of the Moynihan Report contained rather dry, factual information. But the whole framework was in the form of "A Case for National Action," as was suggested by the subtitle. This was clearly shown in the introductory comments of the report, which included the following statements:

The United States is approaching a new crisis in race relations....

In this new period the expectations of the Negro Americans will go beyond civil rights. Being Americans, they will now expect that in the near future equal opportunities for them as a group will produce roughly equal results, as compared with other groups. This is not going to happen. Nor will it happen for generations to come unless a new and special effort is made....

Indices of dollars of income, standards of living, and years of education deceive. The gap between the Negro and most other groups in American society is widening.

The fundamental problem, in which this is most clearly the case, is that of family structure. The evidence—not final, but powerfully persuasive—is that the Negro family in the urban ghettos is crumbling....

Measures that have worked in the past, or would work for most groups in the present, will not work here. A national effort is required that will give a unity of purpose to the many activities of the Federal government in this area, directed to a new kind of national goal: the establishment of a stable Negro family structure.

The report was circulated among government officials in March of 1965. Its ideas were included in a speech made by President Johnson at Howard University on June 4. In fact, Moynihan had an opportunity to review a draft of this speech ("To Fulfill These Rights") and made further suggestions for it. In the speech, sometimes considered the high water mark of Great Society rhetoric, the president called for new measures to address America's problems of racial inequality, including some that would become known as "affirmative action."

Only in August was the Moynihan Report released to the public—after major riots had occurred in the Watts area of Los Angeles. The riots provided an inevitable context for the reception of the report. For some, they provided evidence to support the main points Moynihan had made about a new crisis in race relations. For others, including probably most white Americans, the riots soured the appeal of anything associated with civil rights or other actions which might provide special help for black communities. From this point of view, the report, even when read, tended to be discounted.

Much more disquieting to Moynihan was the reception by liberal intellectuals, including most black social scientists. They considered the report insulting to black Americans. To suggest that an inferior family structure was a chief cause of the lack of black progress was to leave white America relatively blameless, they believed. And it tended, they further suggested, only to enhance undesirable stereotypes about blacks. Some saw it less as an exercise in social science than a piece of anti-black propaganda. To read such evaluations of his work from people he respected was a source of bitter disappointment for Moynihan.[10]

But Moynihan was no longer part of the Johnson administration when the Moynihan Report was released. He resigned on July 18 in order to run for the job of president of the City Council of New York. Caught between the Johnson and Kennedy factions within the administration, Moynihan found the president's attitude increasingly cool to him personally. He sought to escape by running for mayor of New York, but found that he could not get the support for such a campaign at this time. Instead, he was put on the slate for City Council president—and lost in the September primaries. He then found himself without a job either in Washington or New York, just when he was faced with increasingly bitter criticism over the Moynihan Report.

But academia came to the rescue at this point. Moynihan spent the 1965-66 academic year as a fellow in the Center for Advanced Studies at Wesleyan University. After a pleasant year there, he was invited to Cambridge to become director of the Joint Center for Urban Studies of Harvard and MIT. He remained affiliated with Harvard from then until 1977, when he became a U.S. senator from New York.

Nixon's Man

Being back in academia gave Moynihan more time to reflect about what was going on in American society in the hectic years of the 1960s. In his position as an urban studies director, he promoted a careful examination of social science findings about urban problems. For example, he led a searching seminar of top scholars on "The Coleman Report," an ambitious study following the Civil Rights Act of 1964 designed to examine the causes and effects of educational inequality. The voluminous evidence suggested different things to different people, but most were surprised with how little the effects of schools were found to be in promoting educational achievement as compared to effects of family backgrounds. This made old liberals such as Moynihan more modest about the likely effects of government action in solving America's most pressing social problems.

Also, Moynihan was changing in what he saw as the priorities for political action. In 1967 he could speak to the Americans for Democratic Action (a leading liberal group) with questions about the traditional liberal values, suggesting that the promotion of stable public order may be more important now than liberal agendas for social change. More and more he was associating with scholars that were called "neo-conservative," such as those who (as did Moynihan) contributed to Irving Kristol's new journal, *The Public Interest*. While he still called himself a Democrat (Moynihan had supported Robert F. Kennedy's bid for the presidency in early 1968), he was clearly becoming more critical of the Great Society initiatives than he had been earlier.

Although he did not support Nixon for president in 1988, Moynihan was surprised to find himself quoted in some of that candidate's speeches. At least Nixon speech writers were following Moynihan's increased skepticism about what the federal government could do to provide immediate resolution for persisting social problems. Even more surprised was he when Nixon, just after his election, made a point of trying to enlist him into his new team of White House advisors. It was not just some low-level position that Nixon offered; Moynihan was to be a top advisor for domestic affairs, somewhat parallel to the position offered to Henry Kissinger for foreign policy. He would be given the title of counselor to the president and provide leadership for a special cabinet-level task force on urban affairs. To the dismay of many of his friends, Moynihan decided to accept Nixon's offer.

Welfare reform, including national standards of support to apply in all states, was an early policy priority Moynihan proposed to Nixon. He followed this with what was to be known as the Family Security Plan, which included the feature of special tax allowances for low-income families (in effect, a negative income tax—where the poorest families would receive funds at tax time rather than have to pay income taxes). Although only parts of this proposal actually achieved Congressional action, Moynihan was able to convince President Nixon to support some rather far-reaching proposals for new domestic policies.

Moynihan developed a good relationship with the president. However, after about a year his influence began to wane in comparison to other advisors, and ultimately John Ehrlichman took over the operational leadership in the White House for domestic policies. Although he was offered a post as ambassador to the United Nations, Moynihan chose to go back to Harvard when his two-year leave for government service came to an end. He continued, however, to serve as a part-time consultant to the president and as a member of the United Nations delegation.

Moynihan found many of his colleagues at Harvard less than enthusiastic about the role he had played in Nixon's White House, especially after the Nixon presidency began to unravel in 1973. A special item of controversy was the "benign neglect" memo he had written to Nixon in January of 1970. Although intended as a general assessment of current race relations which included positive comments about Negro progress, the memo was most noted for the passage which suggested that "The time may have come when the issue of race could benefit from a period of 'benign neglect.'" Moynihan had then continued: "The subject has been too much talked about. The forum has been too much taken over by hysterics, paranoids and boodlers on all sides. We may need a period in which Negro progress continues and racial rhetoric fades." When parts of this memo were leaked to the press, Moynihan and Nixon were quickly condemned for their insensitivity to American blacks. The very phrase "benign neglect" for many seemed to typify the attitude of the Nixon administration on civil rights issues, and Moynihan, his early domestic advisor, was given a good share of the blame for this.[11]

Moynihan, after an interlude at Harvard, was ready once again to take on a role of governmental service. This opportunity came in the form of an appointment to be the American ambassador to India. He and his wife went to New Delhi for two years, 1973-75, during which he served to improve American-Indian relations in important ways. This was followed by a second offer to become the American ambassador to the United Nations, which this time he accepted. In the UN, Moynihan distinguished himself as a strong supporter of Israel against an attempt to equate Zionism with racism and as a vocal critic of the power of third world nations in UN political affairs. Henry Kissinger, then Secretary of State, found it increasingly difficult to work with his rather free-speaking United Nations representative, and Moynihan, perceiving this, tendered his resignation early in 1976. Apparently he would again be going back to Harvard, from which his second leave of absence was coming to an end.

Indeed, Moynihan did return to Harvard in the spring of 1976, but within a year he had entered into a completely new role—that of United States senator from New York.

The Senator

Moynihan had at first resisted suggestions he might run for the Senate, but he failed to find Harvard satisfying the political interests that had become central for his career. In June, he announced his entry into the Democratic primary for that fall's election. In September, he narrowly led Bella Abzug and several others in the voting, and in November, he easily defeated the Republican candidate. His campaign had not been a well ordered one (with Liz, his wife, taking over much of the leadership to avoid complete chaos), but in the end he was successful. Three more times he ran again for the same office, with generally increasing support—and with Liz Moynihan becoming more seasoned in managing his campaigns.

At last gaining an elective office, Moynihan moved energetically to assume his role as a United States senator. He sought good relations with Democratic Senate leaders to gain membership on the powerful Finance Committee, ultimately becoming the chairman on that group. On such subcommittees as those for international trade, social security and family policy, and taxation, he soon made his imprint on legislation. He also was originally assigned to the Committee on Environment and Public Works, and later he served on committees for foreign relations, the budget, and intelligence.

Moynihan was especially active in legislation that brought federal funds to New York. Very quickly he helped obtain special support to underwrite the debts of New York City. He worked for changes in transportation legislation to provide more funds for urban mass transit in general, and he helped provide billions of dollars for specific projects in the state of New York. He pointed out that New York had been grossly underfunded in comparison to its federal tax contributions (challenging past methods of accounting that treated transfers in New York banks as funds going to New York), thus clearing the way for more special pleading for New York projects.

There can be little doubt that Moynihan supported New York interests throughout his twenty-four years in the Senate. But he also emphasized serving the nation as a whole. During his re-election campaign of 1982 he said: "The Senators are representatives of states in the American constitutional system. They are also United States Senators." Both of these facts, he felt, provide the basis of obligations for a member of the Senate.[12]

Given his recent service to the Nixon and Ford administrations, there was some concern with Moynihan's credentials as a Democrat when he first took his seat in the Senate. He had been critical of the liberal agenda of many of his former colleagues and was seen as more conservative than most of his party. But he easily put on the Democratic mantle for purposes of his Senate work, and more and more returned to some of the main themes of his former liberalism. However, he worked with less concern for party labels or ideological currents than with the substance of proposed legislation. Welfare reform, tax policy, transportation systems, urban planning, public buildings, crime control—these were a few of the general areas in which his expertise became well known and incorporated into important legislation.

Although most noted for his work on domestic issues, Moynihan also had a strong interest in foreign affairs. This was subdued when he worked for presidents Kennedy, Johnson, and Nixon—though he was a generally silent internal critic of the war in Vietnam. It came to full flower in his work as an ambassador—first to India, and then to the United Nations—and continued throughout his Senate career. He was consistently anti-communist and generally favored a hard line against Soviet interests. But he was also oddly-prescient about the demise of the Soviets and of dangers inherent in the disintegration of their system. He had a ready skepticism about the moralistic pretensions of nation states—especially those of the Third World—but he did see important moral imperatives behind foreign policy. A world of democratic values was always for him an underlying goal, just as was a strong respect for international law one of the chief ingredients of the way a major nation should act.

As a senator, Moynihan served under four Presidents, though "served under" hardly fits to describe his relationships with them. He had many differences with Jimmy Carter, who found Moynihan one of the most difficult members of Congress to work with. His respect for Reagan was even less, and helped Moynihan to solidify his status as a Democrat in opposition. Much closer was he to the first George Bush—whose wife, Barbara, was an even closer friend of Liz Moynihan. Then came Bill Clinton, with whom relations were uneven.

Moynihan was on important committees for Clinton's legislative agenda, but he failed to fall easily in line with administration proposals. For example, Moynihan early thought health care reform to be the wrong issue to make central and was highly critical of the plan Clinton put forward. He would have preferred a stronger focus on welfare reform, yet when Clinton later made that his cause, Moynihan was dismayed at the radical way in which the federal government withdrew from welfare support. When the issue of impeachment arose in Clinton's second term, Moynihan was among those senators who were most critical of the president's moral behavior. But in the end, he would not go along with his removal from office. He saw it as ultimately a Constitutional issue. He said, in the dramatic conclusion to his speech in the Senate: "Censure him by all means. He will be gone in less than two years. But do not let his misdeeds put in jeopardy the Constitution we are sworn to uphold and defend."[13]

When Moynihan decided not to seek re-election to his Senate seat in 2000, the person who emerged as his successor was Hillary Clinton.

He gave her his strong endorsement, then retired from the maelstrom of public controversy. His retirement turned out to be relatively brief, for he died at age seventy-six on March 26, 2003, following complications from a ruptured appendix.

The Social Scientist as Politician

There is no standard way of becoming a politician in America. Some men and women come out of political families. Others come into politics after achieving success in a business or profession, with lawyers especially common in legislative assemblies. Some social scientists dabble in politics, but seldom does one become a full-fledged politician or—as in the case of Moynihan—one who treats politics as "a distinguished calling."[14]

In looking back on his own career, Moynihan has said that "almost everything that has happened to me has taken place by chance." It is true that much of his career has seemed to be shaped by chance encounters and by well-timed special opportunities. But one must also note how Moynihan repeatedly rose to whatever occasion might present itself.[15]

Governor Harriman needed staff help, and Pat Moynihan knew the person that the governor had chosen to head his staff. But it was up to Moynihan to show the social and intellectual talents needed to help the governor. Later, personal acquaintances led to a staff position in President Kennedy's Department of Labor, but it was Moynihan who turned this job into a leading voice for Great Society efforts of President Johnson. His opportunity to serve in Nixon's White House seemed to come out of the blue, but he applied his considerable skills to this work—and to serving President Ford in roles of international leadership. He gained his position in the United States Senate after winning the 1976 primary by an extremely narrow margin, but once in the Senate he could remake his position to fit his own character—and achieved reelection for another three terms.

Moynihan's academic career also had many fortuitous junctures—from when he first went to college to when he established himself at Harvard. Personal friendships had a great deal to do with his appointments at Syracuse, Wesleyan, and Harvard; but he also took on the role of an intellectual with gusto and served these universities well. Still, when the opportunity presented itself, Moynihan usually chose public service over academia. He was both a scholar and a politician—but the pull of politics seemed in the end generally stronger than that of the academy.

But Moynihan the politician never extinguished Moynihan the social scientist. He was at his best when thinking through the social implications of public policies—under the guidance of whatever research might be available. Sometimes he had to provide his own research, as in his report on black families in America, and often his interpretations were controversial. But he did at least do his best to consider social science findings when dealing with the issues of public policy.

Interestingly, Moynihan saw no particular priority for policy proposals that come from social scientists. He held that: "The role of social science lies not in the formulation of social policy, but in the measurement of its results." Here the objectivity of social research should be used to help us know just what effects we are creating by particular policies. Moynihan emphasized this critical function of social science in his reflections on the Johnson administration's anti-poverty campaign: "Government, especially liberal government, that would attempt many things very much needs the discipline of skeptical and complex intelligence repeatedly inquiring 'What do you mean?' and 'How do you know?'" This, he believed, is where social science comes into its own as a special asset for democratic government.[16]

Pat Moynihan eludes the most common ideological labels applied in American politics. He was early generally recognized as among the "liberals," but clearly he moved in a more conservative direction when he served Nixon and sought his own rather independent career as a senator. Although a life-long Democrat, he was not narrowly partisan, and his most important contributions as a senator depended on his ability to work across party lines. He eschewed appeals to ethnic politics; however, he recognized the importance of ethnicity and never had any hesitation in identifying himself as an Irish Catholic. He held firmly to core values—such as the central assumptions of American democracy and the importance of families for the general welfare of society—but he could be quite flexible in the way he worked to implement these values with specific government actions. He was, after all, a politician, and he enjoyed the give and take of the political arena.

As a scholar, Moynihan also failed to fit the usual labels. What, after all, was his field? His dissertation was in labor history. In his teaching, he served at various times as professor in government, education, and urban studies. His special niche seemed to be where social science dealt with issues of public policy. This, of course, naturally fit with his service in government.

Moynihan the politician never completely separated himself from Moynihan the social scientist. Sometimes it made for a rather unusual mixture, but he developed a combined career that satisfied himself and came to be supported by many voters.[17]

Part 5

Conclusions

12

Masters of Social Science

The Masters

Our review of the lives and contributions of the eleven twentieth-century social scientists whom we have designated as "masters" has grouped them into three main categories. Some of our masters moved well beyond the category we selected for them, but at least our categories have served to illustrate something of the main contexts of social science work. Let us now remind ourselves of these three main contexts.[1]

The Context of Discovery

In the final section of our chapter on Louis and Mary Leakey, we referred to "the context of discovery" as involving a variety of general features. First of all were the features of the person or persons making a notable discovery. In the case of the Leakeys, we noted especially the skill and persistence with which they worked, though they also were extremely fortunate in their selection of places to look for their evidences of early humans in East Africa. We also made a point of considering the broader community of scientists which is involved in the process of discovery. The Leakeys needed funds to support their field work and skilled workers to carry out their excavations. They were especially sensitive to the kinds of publicity which would make possible this support, and they carefully organized the teams necessary for digging their sites and cataloging what was there found. Then there was the painstaking reporting of their findings so that others would know exactly what had been discovered. This presupposed a group of scientists with a special interest in the area of research involved; their attention was essential in providing motivation for the detailed work required.

Of course, even our greatest discoverers occasionally neglected to pay proper attention to some of the features we have just mentioned. We have seen how Louis Leakey, in some of his early discoveries at Kanam and

Kanjera, failed to provide suitable documentation for his findings. This raised questions about the quality of his fieldwork, leading the Leakeys to be extra careful about their documentation in the future. We have also seen how Margaret Mead had some of her early findings about Samoa questioned by other anthropologists. What she had found in her early study was subject to confirmation (or revision) by the work of others. Thus the broader network of the scientific community—especially those sharing special fields of interest—becomes part of the discovery process. This network serves to validate and recognize—but also to revise—the contributions of our great discoverers.

Some of the great discoveries in the social sciences have been of specific and concrete facts. Louis and Mary Leakey exemplify this kind of work. Others have involved more general patterns. The work of Margaret Mead was not so important for any specific artifact she found as for the patterns of culture she was able to document. This is a broader kind of discovery than those for which the Leakeys gained recognition.

Another type of discovery involved the basic laws of behavior sought by B.F. Skinner. The careful measurement of facts was important here, but the way they were patterned was even more interesting. It was the recurrent patterns of behavior that he and his associates so carefully documented that provided the basic discoveries of operant conditioning. What is especially different in this work is its experimental nature—the designing of controlled experiments to test key ideas and their applications. This requires a special contingent of social scientists interested in a given area of laboratory research—in Skinner's case a group of psychologists who specialized in the study of operant conditioning.

The Context of Theory Building

The context of theory building in the social sciences is similar to that of discovery in important respects. In both cases there is room for highly individualized contributions. Also, the community of scientists plays a central role for both. However, there are also significant differences between these two contexts.

The persistence with which a discoverer pursues truth in the empirical world has its counterpart in the way a theorist pursues truth among ideas. Ideas are not so explicitly true as are the facts in an empirical situation; rather, their truth lies within their relationship to other ideas. Logical consistency becomes a chief criterion of validity for the theorist. Of course, how this is manifested varies from theorist to theorist.

For John Dewey it was ultimately the world of experience that provided the test of truth, though logical reflection was a central part of the process. For Talcott Parsons the ultimate empirical world appeared more distant, behind the clouded array of formal conceptualizations. For Kenneth Boulding there was both the appeal of formal thinking and a respect for the more commonsense world, depending on the task he found at hand. But for all of these social scientists, reflecting upon ideas provided the central activity of their work.

Theory building involves the careful use of concepts, put together to establish structures of thought. Dewey covered the full range of philosophy with his reflections on the nature of thought and experience. Ethics, education, aesthetics, religion, and social action were all included among the frameworks of his pragmatic philosophy. Parsons was much more limited in his focus on social theory, though here he spared no effort to formulate systematic structures of ideas common to the main fields of social science. Boulding, as did Parsons, made strong use of systems theory as he sought the integration of the social sciences—following his earlier contributions to the science of economics.

Each of our master theorists has been identified with a central set of ideas. For Dewey it was the way thought is rooted in experience, with adjustment to a social environment the key element of that experience. The concept of a social system seemed to provide the central theme for Parsons. For Boulding the fundamental unity of the social sciences posed the great theme for the last half of his career, after making the science of economics his home during his early decades as a social scientist.

The Context of Social Reform

Social science can be justified as a pursuit of theory and research simply for the sake of understanding. But the issue of its usefulness for society also cries for special attention. In part, of course, its usefulness depends on the adequacy of empirical and theoretical foundations. Careless work is not likely to be of much use. But there is also the matter of applying the social sciences to the basic questions about society; some of our masters of social science have made this their special concern.

We have identified four of our masters of social science as significant especially for their social reform contributions. These are Gunnar and Alva Myrdal, C. Wright Mills, and Daniel Patrick Moynihan. This does not mean that others have not also made important contributions to social reform (Margaret Mead, John Dewey, and Kenneth Boulding come especially to mind), but for these four masters social science became focused on issues of social reconstruction.

We have selected our masters to illustrate three general approaches to social reform. We have described Gunnar and Alva Myrdal as representing a social engineering model. They pursued systematic research on central problems of human society (such as race relations, world poverty, and the East-West arms race), searching for tools that might be applied to the alleviation of such problems. Using funds from private foundations and international agencies, they directed major research programs, and they eagerly sought the implications of their research for how changes may be made in society.

A second social reform style we have illustrated is that of the social rebel. Of course, it is not rebellion as such that is important here, but the critical stance toward the social order that a social scientist may embody. We have chosen to describe C. Wright Mills as especially this kind of social scientist. He could coolly survey the institutions of American society to suggest how they failed to work for the welfare of common citizens. Although not himself greatly involved in programs of social action, he could provide a critical base for those who were pursuing specific reforms.

Finally, we have sought to explore the life of a social scientist who made his primary contributions in the political arena. Though he was both a social scientist and a politician, it is in the latter role that Daniel Patrick Moynihan is best known. We have seen the close connection between the two sides of his career as he embodied the social scientist as politician. He also illustrated a great variety of political roles (idea man, report writer, program administrator, presidential advisor, international ambassador, and legislator) in which the insights of social science might be applied.

Social Science and the Habit of Truth

We now turn our attention to several general considerations about the nature of social science. We do this by giving attention first to what we call "the habit of truth," then consider the role of reason and the legacy of the Enlightenment, followed by a brief discussion of the special issue of subjectivity. We will then conclude this final chapter with a few speculations about the future.

The story of social science is to a large extent the story of the growth of the empirical spirit in the modern world. We have come to see the world around us as a frontier of facts to be identified and catalogued. This increasingly applies not just to the natural world, but also to the world of human nature. Human society itself has become something that we seek to study through systematic observation and analysis.

The empirical spirit leads us not just to search for facts but also to uncover their sometimes hidden meanings. We seek not only to demonstrate what is generally known, but also to identify new truths. This in part is the achievement of great individuals—such as our masters of social science—but it is even more a product of that community of scientists formed through intellectual exchange. This happens for all the branches of human knowledge. New discoveries, new theories, and new applications are proposed and discussed within the community of scientists. Gradually they take root, as the body of each of the fields of science grows and develops.

"The habit of truth" is the phrase that one philosopher of science, Jacob Bronowski, has used to refer to this spirit of empirical inquiry. He has characterized the foundation of this drive for truth as the "habit of testing and correcting the concept by its consequences in experience." This he saw as one of the central themes of modern Western civilization—"the spring within the movement" of our modern world, he has called it.[2]

Modern social science has emerged during the last two and a half centuries as a product of this growing empirical spirit. But it has not been guided by just the search for objective facts in the world around us. There are also ideological frameworks that have guided our examination of the facts. The spirit of rationalism has been such a framework in the development of social science, and we have had occasion to point to the influence of this among many of our masters

The Enlightenment Legacy

We have sketched the modern quest for social science as beginning with the Enlightenment of the eighteenth century. We have used Condorcet as our key example of this beginning. It was Condorcet who insisted that the progressive growth of human knowledge and the ultimate improvement of human society are the inevitable results of the development of human reason.

Note well the ambitious task here assigned to human reason. Through reason we can come to know the truth about the world as it is; but reason serves not only to tell us "what is" but also "what ought to be." There is a fundamental structure in nature that, once grasped, helps us better use the physical world for improving our lives. Likewise, there is a fundamental structure in human nature and human society, which, once grasped, will help us create a more livable society. This structure includes basic truths such as man's "natural rights" and the fundamental claims of human equality. By correctly perceiving this basic structure, we can use it to guide our reconstruction of the social order.

Condorcet was not alone in expressing this great faith in human reason. Americans find in their own *Declaration of Independence* a similar philosophy (based on "certain unalienable rights," in Thomas Jefferson's famous words). This faith of the Age of Enlightenment has continued down to the present day. The experience of the last two centuries may have left us less optimistic about the fruits of reason than what may be found in Condorcet's eighteenth-century vision; but the spirit that inspired him still lives. It remained alive in Auguste Comte's formulation of a general social science in the nineteenth century, and it is to be found, explicitly or implicitly, in many of the twentieth-century masters we have discussed in our earlier chapters.

The basic assumption that the study of human behavior and society is to be guided by a carefully reasoned examination of evidence is at the heart of all social science. Beyond that, the assumption that this knowledge can usefully be applied to improve society has general assent. However, views vary in the extent to which this may be guided by an impartial reason; there is also the recognition that social changes come through the manipulations by special interest groups, through emotional appeals that give little attention to reasoned discourse, or, sometimes, through brute force.

Among our "masters" may be found a variety of expressions of key Enlightenment themes. Most embody them in their work without drawing them out into explicit philosophies. In a few cases we find more explicit statements of the way reason should guide the quest for social knowledge. We may mention in particular three perspectives which, in different ways, reflect key ideological themes of the Enlightenment. We call these the perspectives of (a) radical empiricism; (b) analytical realism; and (c) social constructionism.

What we term "radical empiricism" places its emphasis on the accumulation of objective facts. "Objective" here is a key word, for only as we can clearly demonstrate our evidence to one another, according to this perspective, can it be effectively used for social science. Then we may gradually build generalizations of these facts that have the status of scientific laws. Ultimately, we may be able to use these laws for engineering new frameworks for human society.

Among our masters, B.F. Skinner most clearly represents this pattern of thought. His behaviorism is a demand for objective evidence, his laws of learning are generalizations from experimental evidence, and his vision clearly includes the application of such laws to the systematic control of human behavior. Of course, critics have seen his view of behavior as too impersonal and his image of human society as overly individualistic; but certainly the main themes of his work show a strong impact of ideals of the Age of Reason.

"Analytical realism" is a term used by Talcott Parsons to represent another style of work. Far from the behaviorism of Skinner, this approach is centered in theoretical reflection. The theories generated are pursued through carefully reasoned discourse. Their ultimate purpose is to clarify the real world in which we live, even though it may be represented in highly abstract terms. The remaking of this world may sometimes be an ultimate objective, but simply trying to understand it is the primary purpose.

Of course, Parsons is our strongest embodiment of this approach, though behind him we also have Max Weber's work. Weber's use of ideal types and his quest for a "value-free" basis for social science are important elements which Parsons and others have used. While critics may see such work as overlaid with abstract jargon, those theorists who operate within such a tradition may see it as representing the highest achievements of human reason in social science.

We use the term "social constructionism" to represent the approach that sees human reason itself as growing out of a social process. Reason, in this view, is not some ready-made structure of thought, but it derives from the experience of testing out our ideas in action. Through our shared experience with others, certain ideas come to be seen as valid and certain ways of dealing with ideas come to be seen as reasonable. Thus we construct, together with one another, the foundations of human reason, which can then guide us onward to the reconstruction of society.

John Dewey is, of course, our best example of social constructionism. His analysis of human behavior and society was systematically based on human reason. But he also had a theory to clarify the nature of reason and how it emerged in human experience. In this he went a step beyond his precursors in the Age of Enlightenment, though his general philosophy was of the same basic pattern.

We have just mentioned some of the legacies of the Age of Enlightenment for twentieth century social scientists. We could mention other individuals as further examples. For example, the bedrock values of reason and freedom for C. Wright Mills were very much products of the same philosophy, and Gunnar Myrdal was quite explicit in making a connection between the ideals of the Age of Enlightenment and his own study of American race relations. It might be assumed, therefore, that Enlightenment ideals (despite their varied manifestations) might provide the central ideology of modern social science. That, however, might be claiming too much.

Some of our masters have led us to at least a few doubts about the faith in human progress that so characterized the Enlightenment. The cynicism of C. Wright Mills about trends in modern society would be hard to recognize as an example of Enlightenment thinking; and Alva Myrdal's devastating analysis of the nuclear arms race certainly did not bear witness to the efficacy of rational thought for twentieth-century international relations. Further qualifications of Enlightenment thinking may be found in the work of Daniel Patrick Moynihan and Kenneth Boulding.

While not taking direct issue with Enlightenment ideals, Moynihan showed a skepticism about the extent to which people are ruled by reason. The strength of ethnicity in the modern world shows that individual interests and economic forces are not sufficient to explain political behavior and, he further suggested, the political process of modern democracy is much more complicated than what can be captured by simple images of rational debate. Further, he came to mistrust the instincts of "liberals" (though he once had been seen as among them) who were too idealistic about how social change might take place. Since he saw many of his fellow social scientists as among these liberals, he came to question their competence for formulating social policies. Policies should come out of the general political process, he felt, not from the minds of social science experts. This led him to make a basic distinction between the formulation of policy (where social scientists had no special expertise) and the evaluation of policy (where social science research should be of critical importance). All in all, this is hardly the kind of thinking we would expect from Condorcet, should he be reborn as a senator from New York!

Then there is Kenneth Boulding. While much of his work (especially his early work in economics) was a model of rational precision, he never enthroned reason in quite the same way as did many of his social science colleagues. He was a poet as well as a scientist, and his social science work often followed wide leaps of the imagination. Even more specifically, his religious roots led him to look beyond empirical evidence for fundamental ethical commitments. His vision of a world at peace was therefore not so much the legacy of human reason (though he contributed wholeheartedly to the scientific work of peace research) as it was a result of essentially religious sentiments.

The Issue of Subjectivity

Social science is sometimes held to be fundamentally different from natural science in the way it may blur the subject-object dichotomy. The data of social science are in a sense part of the observer, it is often held, and this makes complete objectivity impossible.

It is possible to oppose this claim by saying that no fundamental distinction need be seen here. Scientists are always parts of the universe that they observe, with the very process of observation becomes part of data recorded. On the other hand, systematic controls may allow even an observer's self-knowledge to be recorded in a thoroughly objective manner. The behaviorism of B.F. Skinner offers a notable example. By applying a thoroughly rigorous and systematic method to examine our own behavior, it may be seen as much a part of the objective world as would apply to any natural phenomena.

But most social scientists do at least see some important differences. More often than in the natural sciences, the social scientist appears to be part of what he or she is studying. A further complication lies in the way the phenomena we study may change their natures just because they are being studied. That persons and groups studied may learn what is said about them by social scientists may induce them to change their behavior in important ways. Sometimes this may invalidate the observations initially (and correctly) made, as people change in response to what is said about them. At other times, social scientists may be part of a self-fulfilling prophecy. By presenting their generalizations to those they study, they may make their subjects even more likely to continue in their described patterns. Does not "science" say that such behavior is only natural?

Most social scientists do not see the idea of subject-object convergence in their work as a critical problem. In practical terms, they treat their human subject matter as something separate from themselves. When they find themselves getting involved in some major way, they seek special techniques to help them maintain their objectivity. This seems to represent the mainstream of social science thinking. But some of our masters have dealt with this issue differently. Here we may mention in particular the frameworks suggested by Gunnar Myrdal and John Dewey.

Myrdal was among those who rejected the idea of a "value-free" social science. There are always values inherent in those persons and institutions we study, as well as in our social science approaches to their study. The human world is in large part a world of values, and the "facts" we record as social scientists should not seek to neutralize this larger truth. This, however, does not suggest we should resign ourselves to the whims of personal subjectivity. Social scientists do have important work to do that involves careful analysis of facts; but even more important is their work in relating these to the implicit and explicit values people carry with them in their institutions. By helping to make clear these values (for example, the values of "the American Creed" in relation to American patterns of racial discrimination) social scientists may have special opportunities to assist in social reconstruction.

Even more basic was John Dewey's handling of the subjectivity-objectivity issue. With Dewey, as with Myrdal, facts are always related to larger values; this assumption naturally set the stage for Dewey's social reform commitments. But Dewey cut deeper by discussing issues of the fundamental nature of human knowledge. By seeing our knowledge as grounded in experience, and seeing that experience largely collective in nature, Dewey developed an epistemology that avoided a simple subject-object dichotomy. His pragmatic view of truth as what may be tested in action led to the view that our scientific objectivity was at best a temporary expedient. The fundamental processes of knowing our world are inherently a part of our social life in that world.

Not all of our masters would agree with the positions presented by Myrdal or Dewey for resolving the subjectivity-objectivity issue. Most, however, would accept that there is a special challenge for social science to develop objective means of analysis in pursuing the understanding of a world that includes ourselves as observers.

The Future

We have not tried in this book to give a systematic review of the main trends of twentieth-century social science, and we will not do so now. However, as we see the twenty-first century unfolding, we are bound to wonder how the future might compare with the past. For this question the present writer can claim no special expertise. The brief comments which follow are purely speculative.

There appears no reason to believe that we have reached the end of our masters of social science. We will continue to have great men and women who will push forward the frontiers of our knowledge. Further, there is no reason to believe that any of what we have treated as the three main contexts of social science (discovery, theory, and social reform) will be any less important in the future.

There no doubt will be differences in the degree to which social science disciplines, and the particular fields within them, will be emphasized. This will depend on the demands of society as well as on the growth of new areas of knowledge. For example, it would appear that criminology will be a growth area for some decades to come due to the vast sums of money governments are spending in this direction. And the study of neurological and genetic roots of social behavior will continue to grow with new findings in the sciences of neurology and human genetics. Studies of social organization will increasingly recognize the great variety of electronic linkages between people, changing the nature of social interaction for many purposes of sociological analysis.

Despite all these likely developments, it is hard to see that there will not remain the quest for a general social science of human society and behavior. The universities may divide themselves into departments based on conventional social science disciplines, or even their sub-specialties, but there will still be behind the full range of the social sciences a unity of basic questions. What are the bedrock assumptions we must make about human nature and behavior? What is at the foundation of human society and the manner in which it changes? And how do we evaluate the changes we observe in our present social institutions? These are questions of social science, requiring insights beyond a single discipline.

There is at least a reasonable hope that we will find new discoverers, theorists, and social reformers that will have as strong an impact on social science as the "masters" we have reviewed in this book.

Notes

Chapter 1

1. M.F. Argo, as quoted by Schapiro (1934), p. 67. Schapiro's book is probably the best single source on the life and thought of Condorcet.
2. Condorcet's summary of central ideas of the *philosophes* is found in his *Progress of the Human Mind*, quoted by Schapiro, p. 43.
3. Quoted by Schapiro, p. 73.
4. The description of Condorcet's wife is quoted by Schapiro, p. 75.
5. These personal descriptions by contemporaries are quoted by Schapiro, p. 91.
6. Quoted by Schapiro, p. 101.
7. The title of Condorcet's masterpiece in French was *Esquisse d'un tablelau historique des progres de l'espirit humain*. It has been translated into English in several ways, though perhaps its most common citation is as *Progress of the Human Mind*.
8. Quotations here are from Condorcet's *Progress*, as included in Bierstedt (1959), p. 166.
9. In Bierstedt, p. 161.
10. Quoted by Schapiro, p. 106.
11. See, for example, Andrew Coleman's discussion in *Game Theory and Experimental Games* (Coleman, 1982), especially chapter 10.
12. Main sources used for the life and ideas of Auguste Comte have been Barnes (1948), Barnes and Becker (1938), Ellwood (1938), and Timasheff (1955).
13. Quoted by Sokoloff (1961), p. 94.
14. The quoted material here is from Barnes and Becker (1938), p. 567.

Chapter 2

1. Karl Marx's *Das Kapital* was a monumental work for several areas. Here, and in other writings, Marx laid claim to major contributions in history, economics, sociology, and political science. Some of his earlier writings had elements of social psychology as well. Marx was both a theorist and a social activist, using generally historical materials and empirical work reported by others. Though very different in his individualism from the collectivist views of Marx, Herbert Spencer was equally influential in contributing to social science. His evolutionary philosophy (after all, it was he, not Darwin, that first used the phrase "survival of the fittest") served as the basis for his formulations of both psychology and sociology. He, as Marx, used evidence from second-hand sources, but came into his own as a theorist and a proponent of social reform. Other persons who might be mentioned as masters of social science during the late nineteenth or early twentieth centuries include Émile Durkheim, Sigmund Freud, Vilfredo Pareto, and Max Weber. We

will note in later chapters how these leading scholars have influenced some of those whose biographies we include.

Chapter 3

1.   Louis Leakey (1937), p. 32.
2.   We have found Morell (1995) to be our most thorough source on the lives of Louis and Mary Leakey. A good general overview of the field of human evolution may be found in Richard Leakey (1994).
3.   See Morell (1995), p. 309. Mary's full report came out in 1971 with the title of *Oldavai Gorge, Volume 3, Excavations in Beds I and II, 1960-1963*, published by Cambridge University Press.
4.   Mary Leakey's autobiography, *Disclosing the Past* (1984) describes her reactions during their last years together. The quotations are both from p. 140.
5.   Mary Leakey (1984), pp. 214 and 215.
6.   Professor Boswell's views are quoted by Morell, pp. 86 and 92. The ultimate evaluation of the Kanam and Kanjera finds, while still heavily speculative, suggests that Louis Leakey was right in interpreting Kanam Man as very old but still quite human, probably deserving the *Homo* designation. The Kanjera pieces, however, were from sites no older than about 10,000 years. See the footnote on p. 93 of Morell (1995).

Chapter 4

1.   The most complete biography of Margaret Mead is by Jane Howard (1984). See also Bowman-Kruhm (2003).
2.   The quotation above is from Mead (1972), p. 151.
3.   Mead (1928/49).
4.   The above Boas quotation is from the New American Library edition, p. viii.
5.   Mead (1930), p. 19; quoted by Howard (1984), p. 121.
6.   The work among the Omaha is described in Mead (1972), with our quotation from p. 120.
7.   Mead (1935/1950).
8.   The quotation above from *Sex and Temperament* is from the New American Library edition (1950), p. 218. The *Male and Female* quote is from Mead (1949), p. 384.
9.   The above quotations are, respectively, from Mead (1965), p. 1, and Mead (1977), p. 1.
10. Nancy McDowell, as quoted by Howard (1984), p. 430.
11. The quotation is from Howard, pp. 272-273.
12. Quoted by Howard, p. 253.
13. Howard, p. 324.
14. Mead (1960).
15. Freeman (1983).

Chapter 5

1.   Skinner (1970), p. 2.
2.   The quotations here are from Skinner (1970), pp. 2 and 3.
3.   Skinner (1970), p. 5. The earlier quotation about his interest in literature is from Skinner (1976), p. 211.
4.   Skinner (1970), p. 6.
5.   Quoted by Schellenberg (1978), p. 88.

6. Skinner (1972), p. 103.
7. The quotations here are from Skinner (1970), p. 9, and Skinner (1979), p. 5.
8. Skinner (1979), p. 8.
9. The above quotation is from Skinner (1979), p. 59.
10. See Skinner (1938).
11. Skinner (1979), p. 268.
12. Skinner (1957).
13. Skinner (1948). The quotation about this as self-therapy is from Skinner (1970), p. 13.
14. Skinner (1953).
15. Skinner (1970), p. 15.
16. In this final section we will draw heavily upon what earlier appeared in Schellenberg (1978).
17. The quotation here is from Skinner (1972), p. 370.
18. Skinner (1950).
19. Skinner (1971).
20. Quoted in Wiener (1997), p. 179.

Chapter 6

1. We have found Dykhuizen (1973) to be an especially good general source for John Dewey's life and thought.
2. The quotation here is from Dykhuizen (1973), p. 4.
3. The quotation here is from Jane Dewey (1939), p. 21.
4. This comment about James was quoted by Jane Dewey, p. 23.
5. Quoted by Dykhuizen (1973), p. 95.
6. See Dewey (1899) and Dewey (1902). The quotation is from Dewey (1899), p. 49.
7. The quotations here are from Dykhuizen, pp 277 and 278, respectively.
8. Quoted by Jane Dewey (1939), p. 18.
9. Quoted by Dykhuizen, p. 85.
10. See Dewey (1922).
11. The quotation here is from the third edition of *Experience and Nature*, p. xiii.
12. Quoted by Dykhuizen, p. 286.

Chapter 7

1. Although there is an extensive literature on the theories of Talcott Parsons, there is apparently no good general biography to portray his life. There are brief biographical accounts in several books about his ideas—see especially Robertson (1969), Rocher (1975), Hamilton (1983), Camic (1991), Robertson and Turner (1991), Trevaño (2001), and Gerhardt (2002)—and he has furnished some autobiographical reflections in Parsons (1977b). Some biographical information has also been provided by his family, especially by his son Charles Parsons. But the present writer has been surprised at the relative absence of a literature on the life of Talcott Parsons.
2. Quoted by Camic (1991), p. xx.
3. Parsons (1977b), pp. 26-27.
4. See Parsons (1937).
5. See Parsons (1951).
6. See Parsons and Shils (1951), Parsons, Bales, and Shils (1953), Parsons and Bales (1955), and Parsons and Smelser (1956). A good source of early commentary on Parsonian theory (including an extended essay by Parsons himself) is that of Black (1961).

7.   The pattern variables were first fully presented in Parsons and Shils (1951).
8.   The "AGIL" system was first presented in Parsons, Bales, and Shils (1953).
9.   See Parsons (1969), Parsons (1971), and Parsons (1977a).
10.   Parsons (1971), p. 121; quoted by Trevaño (2001), p. lii.
11.   Among many works that have pictured the conservative nature of Parsons' theories,
      see Collins and Makowsky (1972). For the discussion of liberal democratic values
      in Parsons' work, see especially Robertson and Turner (1991) and Gerhardt (2002).
      A good balance of views regarding the contributions of Parsons may be found in
      Trevino (2001).
12.   See Parsons (1977b), p 73.

Chapter 8

1.   Our primary source for Kenneth Boulding's early life are his brief memoirs found
      in Boulding (1980). The passage here is from pp. 4-5. The best general biographi-
      cal source for Boulding is Kerman (1974).
2.   The quotation in this paragraph is from Boulding (1980), p. 9. Quotations in the
      following paragraph are from pp. 15 and 14, respectively.
3.   Boulding (1980), p. 15.
4.   See Boulding (1941).
5.   Quotations here are from Boulding (1980), pp. 18-19 and p. 19.
6.   Boulding (1941).
7.   Boulding (1950), with our quotation from p. ix.
8.   Daniel Fusfeld, quoted by Kerman (1974), p. 33.
9.   See Boulding (1945). The quotation is from Boulding (1980), p. 31.
10.   See Boulding (1958).
11.   Boulding (1958), p. 189.
12.   Quoted by Kerman (1974), p. 124.
13.   See Boulding (1962) and Benoit and Boulding (1963).
14.   Benoit and Boulding (1963), p. ix; quoted by Kerman (1974), pp. 75-76.
15.   See Boulding (1956).
16.   See Boulding (1953) and Boulding (1985).
17.   See Boulding (1973); Boulding, Pfaff, and Pfaff (1973); and Boulding (1984).
18.   Boulding (1989). The final quotation is from p. 250.
19.   For his wide-ranging interests Boulding found himself elected to the presidency
      of the American Association for the Advancement of Science in 1979.
20.   The quotation here is from Kerman (1974), p. 25.

Chapter 9

1.   For our information about the lives of Gunnar and Alva Myrdal, we draw especially
      on Jackson (1990). The quote here is from p. 51. Other sources of biographical
      data include Bok (1991) and Southern (1987).
2.   Quoted by Jackson, p. 75.
3.   Quotations in this paragraph are from Jackson, pp. 56 and 57, respectively.
4.   The quotations here are from Jackson, p. 86.
5.   Jackson, p. 88.
6.   The quotation is from Jackson , p. 149.
7.   The quotations here are from Jackson, p. 159.
8.   Quoted by Jackson, p. 163.
9.   See Gunnar Myrdal (1944).
10.   Quotations are from Myrdal (1944), p. xlvii. Italics in original.

11.   See Alva Myrdal and Viola Klein (1956).
12.   Bok (1991), p. 127.
13.   See Myrdal (1968).
14.   Quoted by Bok (1991), p. 361.
15.   Alva Myrdal (1976), p. 334. Later in a 1982 edition of this book she saw the world situation as "much worse," but she still energetically sought new opportunities for popular awareness and action.
16.   Such was the formal explanation announced in Stockholm when the 1974 prizes were awarded.
17.   Quoted in a news report by the *Boston Globe* on October 14, 1982.
18.   The "battleships" quote above is from Jackson (1990), p. 361.
19.   Jan's writings about his family were put into a different context by the later and more comprehensive biography of Alva written by her daughter (Bok, 1991).
20.   Gunnar Myrdal, "The Place of Values in a World of Facts," Nobel Symposium 14 in Stockholm, September 1969.
21.   Myrdal (1944), p. 1024.

Chapter 10

1.   Mills (1951), pp. 30-31.
2.   The source for this incident (as well as for the quotation in the following paragraph) is Scimecca (1977), p. 9. Other sources for the early life of Mills include Eldridge (1983), Horowitz (1983), Press (1978), and Tilman (1985).
3.   The expressed hope of his father regarding Mills' entry at Texas A & M is from Eldridge (1983), p. 15.
4.   The Ayres quotation is from Tilman (1985), p. 7. The other quotation is from a letter by A. P. Brogan, as found in Horowitz (1983), p. 21.
5.   See Gerth and Mills (1946) and (1953).
6.   The quotation from the article on "social pathologists" is from Press (1978), p. 59. Other information about Mills' work at Wisconsin is primarily from Horowitz (1983).
7.   The above quotation from a letter to Gerth is found in Horowitz, p. 62.
8.   See Mills, Senior, and Goldsen (1950). The Decatur study finally came out in Katz and Lazarsfeld (1955).
9.   See Mills (1948), (1951), and (1956).
10.   Mills (1948), p. 19.
11.   Mills (1951), p. 353.
12.   See Mills (1956).
13.   Mills (1960a), p. 4.
14.   Gerth and Mills (1946) and (1953); and Mills (1951), (1956), and (1959).
15.   Mills (1959), with the quote from p. 18.
16.   The quotations here are both from p. 3.
17.   The quotations in this paragraph are from p. 6, p. 7, and p. 7, respectively.
18.   The quotation on war is from Mills (1959), p. 9.
19.   P. 194.
20.   Mills (1958) and (1960b).
21.   See Mills (1962).
22.   Horowitz (1983), p. 329.

Chapter 11

1.   The best biographical studies of Moynihan are Schoen (1979) and Hodgson (2000). The *New York Times* endorsement is described in Hodgson, pp. 266-270.

2.   Quoted by Hodgson (2000), p. 29.
3.   Quoted by Hodgson, p. 73.
4.   Moynihan's early article on traffic safety appeared in *The Reporter*, 20, no. 9, April 30, 1959, pp. 16-23.
5.   See Glazer and Moynihan (1963). The quotation in the following paragraph is from the second (1970) edition of this book, p. xcvii.
6.   See especially Moynihan (1969b) and (1970).
7.   The FBI quotations are from Hodgson (2000), p. 71.
8.   He later wrote about this issue in Moynihan (1969a).
9.   The Moynihan Report is reproduced on pp. 41-124 of Rainwater and Yancey (1967).
10. The intense controversy over the Moynihan Report is well documented by Rainwater and Yancey (1967).
11. Moynihan's "benign neglect" memo is quoted in Hodgson (2000), p. 158.
12. Quoted by Hodgson (2000), pp. 299-300.
13. Quoted by Hodgson, p. 399.
14. See Katzmann (1998), especially the statement of William Schneider quoted on p. 3.
15. The quotation here is from Hodgson, p. 49.
16. The quotations here are from Moynihan (1969a), pp. 193 (italics in original) and 192, respectively.
17. Wilson (1998), p. 176, has given us the following summary statement on his friend Pat Moynihan: "To me, Pat is the ideal public servant, not because we always agree but because he will follow the facts and even pay, in public money and dashed hopes, to get the facts. If the Senate had a hundred Moynihans, two things would happen: speeches would be a lot better, and the government would be driven by hard facts rather than by empty ideology."

Chapter 12

1.   We will use this note to recognize some of the variations we have found among our eleven masters.

In terms of time, the contributions of our masters have been especially concentrated during the middle half of the twentieth century. However, one (John Dewey) had an active professional life already at the beginning of the century, and another (Daniel Patrick Moynihan) was still active into the twenty-first century.

In terms of physical location, six of the eleven were born in the United States and remained Americans throughout their careers. Two others (Gunnar and Alva Myrdal) were from Sweden, two more were born in England (Kenneth Boulding, who later became an American, and Mary Leakey, who spent most of her productive years in East Africa), and one (Louis Leakey) was born in Kenya and based in East Africa for most of his life. The cosmopolitan nature of this group is greater than these facts would suggest in that nearly all made important contributions outside their home countries. On the other hand, there was a remarkable concentration of professional locations, in that all six Americans had central affiliations with one or the other of two institutions of higher education—Mead, Dewey, and Mills with Columbia Univeristy; and Skinner, Parsons, and Moynihan with Harvard.

Well-recognized social science disciplines with which our masters have been identified include anthropology (Mead), psychology (Skinner), philosophy (Dewey), economics (Boulding and Gunnar Myrdal), and sociology (Parsons and Mills). Paleoanthropology provided a special niche for two others (the Leakeys), with the remaining two (Moynihan and Alva Myrdal) not easily identified with any single discipline. Most had doctoral degrees in the discipline of their primary identification, but the case can be made that this applied to neither Parsons (who began in economics) nor Moynihan (whose doctoral dissertation was in labor history, an area in which he did not later teach). Nor did it apply to the three masters (Mary Leakey, Kenneth Boulding, and Alva Myrdal) who never earned a doctoral degree. Despite whatever disciplinary identification each may have had, it is important to recognize that all our masters made important contributions beyond any home discipline.

A variety of personal styles are also represented by our masters. Some were generally quiet persons who devoted themselves to very careful work. Dewey, Parsons, and Mary Leakey come to mind as examples. On the other hand we have more aggressive or even flamboyant personalities such as those of Mills, Moynihan, or Louis Leakey. Others showed interesting combinations, such as the ambitious but cool efforts of Skinner or Gunnar Myrdal; the constantly driven but widely popular career shown by Margaret Mead; or the gentle and self-deprecating Boulding, who nevertheless had such a bold style of work.

2.	See Bronowski (1965), especially p. 46.

Bibliography

Barnes, Harry Elmer. 1948. "The Social and Political Philosophy of Auguste Comte." In H. E. Barnes (ed.), *An Introduction to the History of Sociology*, pp. 81-109. Chicago: University of Chicago Press.

Barnes, Harry Elmer, and Howard Becker. 1938. *Social Thought from Lore to Science*. Boston: D.C. Heath.

Bateson, Mary Catherine. 1984. *With a Daughter's Eye: A Memoir of Margaret Mead and Gregory Bateson*. New York: William Morrow.

Benoit, Emile, and Kenneth E. Boulding (eds.). 1963. *Disarmament and the Economy*. New York: Harper and Row.

Bierstedt, Robert (ed.). 1959. *The Making of Society: An Outline of Sociology*, Revised edition. New York: Random House.

Black, Max (ed.). 1961. *The Social Theories of Talcott Parsons: A Critical Examination*. Englewood Cliffs, NJ: Prentice-Hall.

Bok, Sissela. 1991. *Alva Myrdal: A Daughter's Memoir*. Reading, MA: Addison Wesley.

Boulding, Kenneth E. 1941. *Economic Analysis*. New York: Harper and Row.

_____. 1945. *The Economics of Peace*. New York: Prentice-Hall.

_____. 1950. *A Reconstruction of Economics*. New York: Wiley.

_____. 1953. *The Organizational Revolution*. New York: Harper.

_____. 1956. *The Image: Knowledge in Life and Society*. Ann Arbor: University of Michigan Press.

_____. 1958. *The Skills of the Economist*. Cleveland, OH: Howard Allen.

_____. 1962. *Conflict and Defense*. New York: Harper.

_____. 1973. *The Economy of Love and Fear: A Preface to Grants Economics*. Belmont, CA: Wadsworth.

_____. 1980. "Memoirs of a Pre-Beatle-Liverpudlian American." In *Beasts, Ballads, and Bouldingisms*, Richard P. Beilock (ed.), pp. 3-23. New Brunswick, NJ: Transaction Publishers.

_____. (ed.). 1984. *The Economics of Human Betterment*. Albany: State University of New York Press.

_____. 1985. *The World as a Total System*. Beverly Hills, CA: Sage Publications.

_____. 1989. *Three Faces of Power*. Beverly Hills, CA: Sage Publications.

Boulding, Kenneth, Martin Pfaff, and Anita Pfaff (eds.) 1973. *Transfers in an Urbanized Economy: Theories and Effects of the Grants Economy*. Belmont, CA: Wadsworth.

Bowman-Kruhm, Mary. 2003. *Margaret Mead: A Biography*. Westport, CT: Greenwood Press.

Bronowski, Jacob. 1965. *Science and Human Values*, revised edition. New York: Harper.

Camic, Charles (ed.). 1991. *Talcott Parsons: The Early Years*. Chicago: University of Chicago Press.

Coleman, Andrew M. 1982. *Game Theory and Experimental Games: The Study of Strategic Interaction*. Oxford: Permagon Press.

Collins, Randall, and Michael Makowsky, 1972. *The Discovery of Society*. New York: Random House.

Dewey, Jane. 1939. "The Biography of John Dewey." In *The Philosophy of John Dewey*, Paul A. Schilpp (ed.), pp. 3-45. Evanston, IL: Northwestern University Press.

Dewey, John. 1899. *The School and Society*. Chicago: University of Chicago Press.

_____.1902. *The Child and the Curriculum*. University of Chicago Press.

_____. 1916. *Democracy and Education: An Introduction to the Philosophy of Education*. New York: Macmillan.

_____. 1922. *Human Nature and Conduct*. New York: Henry Holt.

_____. 1925. *Experience and Nature*. Chicago: Open Court Publishing Company.

_____. 1938a. *Experience and Education*. New York: Macmillan.

_____. 1938b. *Logic: The Theory of Inquiry*. New York: Henry Holt.

Dykhuizen, George. 1973. *The Life and Mind of John Dewey*. Carbondale, IL: Southern Illinois Press.

Eldridge, John. 1983. *C. Wright Mills*. London: Tavistock Publications.

Ellwood, Charles A. 1938. *A History of Social Philosophy*. New York: Prentice-Hall.

Freeman, Derek. 1983. *Margaret Mead and Samoa: The Making and Unmaking of an Anthropological Myth*. Cambridge, MA: Harvard University Press.

Gerhardt, Uta. 2002. *Talcott Parsons: An Intellectual Biography*. Cambridge, UK: Cambridge University Press.

Gerth, Hans, and C. Wright Mills (eds.). 1946. *From Max Weber: Essays in Sociology*. New York: Oxford University Press.

_____. 1953. *Character and Social Structure: The Psychology of Social Institutions*. New York: Harcourt, Brace and Co.

Glazer, Nathan, and Daniel P. Moynihan. 1963. *Beyond the Melting Pot: The Negroes, Puerto Ricans, Jews, Italians, and Irish in New York City*. Cambridge, MA: MIT Press.

Hamilton, Peter. 1983. *Talcott Parsons*. London: Travistock Publications.

Hodgson, Godfrey. 2000. *The Gentleman from New York: Daniel Patrick Moynihan, A Biography*. Boston: Houghton Mifflin.

Horowitz, Irving Louis. 1983. *C. Wright Mills: An American Utopian*. New York: Free Press.

Howard, Jane. 1984. *Margaret Mead: A Life*. New York: Simon and Schuster.

Jackson, Walter A. 1990. *Gunnar Myrdal and America's Conscience: Social Engineering and Racial Liberalism, 1938-1987*. Chapel Hill: University of North Carolina Press.

Katz, Elihu, and Paul F. Lazarsfeld. 1955. *Personal Influence: The Part Played by People in the Flow of Mass Communications*. Glencoe, IL: Free Press.

Katzmann, Robert A. (ed.). 1998. *Daniel Patrick Moynihan: The Intellectual in Public Life*. Baltimore, MD: John Hopkins University Press.

Kerman, Cynthia Earl. 1974. *Creative Tension: The Life and Thought of Kenneth Boulding*. Ann Arbor: University of Michigan Press.

Leakey, Louis S. B. 1937. *White African*. London: Hedder and Stoughton.

_____. 1974. *By the Evidence: Memoirs, 1932-1951*. New York: Harcourt Brace Jovanovich.

Leakey, Mary. 1984. *Disclosing the Past*. Garden City, NY: Doubleday and Company.

Leakey, Richard. 1994. *The Origin of Humankind*. New York: Basic Books.

Mead, Margaret. 1972. *Blackberry Winter: My Earlier Years*. New York: William Morrow.

_____. 1928/1949. *Coming of Age in Samoa*. New York: William Morrow/ New American Library.

_____. 1930. *Growing Up in New Guinea*. New York: William Morrow.

_____. 1935/1950. *Sex and Temperament in Three Primitive Societies*. New York: William Morrow/ New American Library.

_____. 1942. *And Keep Your Powder Dry*. New York: William Morrow.

_____. 1947. *Male and Female: A Study of the Sexes in a Changing World*. New York: William Morrow.

_____. 1960. *New Lives for Old: Cultural Transformation—Manus 1928-1953*. New York: William Morrow.

_____. 1965. *Anthropologists and What They Do*. New York: Franklin Watts.

_____. 1977. *Letters from the Field 1925-1975*. New York: Harper & Row.

Mills, C. Wright. 1948. *The New Men of Power: America's Labor Leaders*. New York: Harcourt, Brace and Co.

_____. 1951. *White Collar: The American Middle Classes*. New York: Oxford University Press.

_____. 1956. *The Power Elite*. New York: Oxford University Press.

_____. 1958. *The Causes of World War III*. New York: Simon & Schuster.

_____. 1959. *The Sociological Imagination*. New York: Oxford University Press.

_____ (ed.). 1960a. *Images of Man: The Classical Tradition in Sociological Thinking*. New York: George Braziller.

_____. 1960b. *Listen, Yankee! The Revolution in Cuba*. New York: McGraw-Hill.

_____. 1962. *The Marxists*. New York: Dell Publishing.

Mills, C. Wright, Clarence Senior, and Rose K. Goldsen. 1950. *The Puerto Rican Journey: New York's Newest Migrants*. New York: Harper and Brothers.

Morell, Virginia. 1995. *Ancestral Passions: The Leakey Family and the Quest for Humankind's Beginnings*. New York: Simon and Schuster.

Moynihan, Daniel P. 1969a. *Maximum Feasible Misunderstanding: Community Action in the War on Poverty*. New York: Free Press.

_____ (ed.). 1969b. *On Understanding Poverty*. New York: Basic Books.

_____ (ed.). 1970. *Toward a National Urban Policy*. New York: Basic Books.

Myrdal, Alva. 1976. *The Game of Disarmament*. New York: Pantheon Books.

Myrdal, Alva, and Viola Klein. 1956. *Women's Two Roles: Home and Work*. London: Routledge & Kegan Paul.

Myrdal, Gunnar. 1944. *An American Dilemma: The Negro Problem and American Democracy*. New York: Harper and Brothers.

_____. 1968. *Asian Drama: An Inquiry into the Poverty of Nations*. New York: Twentieth Century Fund.

Parsons, Talcott. 1937. *The Structure of Social Action*. Glencoe, IL: Free Press.

_____. 1951. *The Social System*. Glencoe, IL: Free Press.

_____. 1969. *Politics and Social Structure*. New York: Free Press.

_____. 1971. *The System of Modern Societies*. Englewood Cliffs, NJ: Prentice-Hall.

_____. 1977a. *The Evolution of Societies*. Englewood Cliffs, NJ: Prentice-Hall.

_____. 1977b. *Social Systems and the Evolution of Action Theory*. New York: Free Press.

Parsons, Talcott., and Robert F. Bales. 1955. *Family, Socialization, and Interaction Process*. Glencoe, IL: Free Press.

Parsons, Talcott, Robert F. Bales, and Edward A. Shils. 1953. *Working Papers in the Theory of Action*. Glencoe, IL: Free Press.

Parsons, Talcott, and Edward A. Shils (eds.). 1951. *Toward a General Theory of Action*. Cambridge, MA: Harvard University Press.

Parsons, Talcott, and Neil J. Smelser. 1956. *Economy and Society*. Glencoe, IL: Free Press.

Press, Howard. 1978. *C. Wright Mills*. Boston: G. K. Hall.

Rainwater, Lee, and William L. Yancey. 1967. *The Moynihan Report and the Politics of Controversy*. Cambridge, MA: MIT Press.

Robertson, Roland. 1969. "Talcott Parsons." In *The Founding Fathers of Social Science*. Timothy Ralston (ed.), pp. 284-300. London: Scolar Press.

Robertson, Roland, and Bryan S. Turner. 1991. *Talcott Parsons: Theorist of Modernity*. London: Sage Publications.

Rocher, Guy. 1975. *Talcott Parsons and American Sociology*. New York: Barnes and Noble.

Schapiro, J. Salwyn. 1934. *Condorcet and the Rise of Liberalism*. New York: Harcourt, Brace.

Schellenberg, James A. 1978. *Masters of Social Psychology*. New York: Oxford University Press.

Schilpp, Paul Arthur (ed.). 1939. *The Philosophy of John Dewey*. Evanston, IL: Northwestern University Press.

Schoen, Douglas. 1979. *Pat: A Biography of Daniel Patrick Moynihan*. New York: Harper & Row.

Scimecca, Joseph A. 1977. *The Sociological Theory of C. Wright Mills*. Port Washington, NY: Associated Faculty Press.

Skinner, B. F. 1938. *The Behavior of Organisms*. New York: Appleton-Century.

_____. 1948. *Walden Two*. New York: Macmillan.

_____. 1950. "Are Theories of Learning Necessary?" *Psychological Review*, 52 (1945), pp. 270-77.

_____. 1953. *Science and Human Behavior*. New York: Macmillan.

_____. 1957. *Verbal Behavior*. New York: Appleton-Century-Crofts.

_____. 1970. "B.F. Skinner, An Autobiography." In *Festschrift for B. F. Skinner*, P.B. Dews, ed., pp. 1-21. New York: Appleton-Century-Crofts.

_____. 1971. *Beyond Freedom and Dignity*. New York: Alfred A. Knopf.

_____. 1972. *Cumulative Record*, 3rd ed. New York: Appleton-Century-Crofts.

_____. 1976. *Particulars of My Life*. New York: Alfred A. Knopf.

_____. 1979. *The Shaping of a Behaviorist*. New York: Alfred A. Knopf.

Sokoloff, Boris. 1961. *The "Mad" Philosopher Auguste Comte*. Westport, CT: Greenwood Press.

Southern, David W. 1987. *Gunnar Myrdal and Black-White Relations: The Use and Abuse of An American Dilemma, 1944-1969*. Baton Rough: Louisiana State University Press.

Tilman, Rick. 1985. *C. Wright Mills: A Native Radical and His American Intellectual Roots*. University Park: Pennsylvania State University Press.

Timasheff, Nicholas S. 1955. *Sociological Theory: Its Nature and Growth*. Garden City, NY: Doubleday.

Treviño, A. Javier (ed.). 2001. *Talcott Parsons Today: His Theory and Legacy in Contemporary Sociology*. Lanham, MD: Rowman and Littlefield. .

Wiener, Daniel N. 1996. *B. F. Skinner: Benign Anarchist*. Boston: Allyn and Bacon.

Wilson, James Q. 1998. "Pat." In *Daniel Patrick Moynihan: The Intellectual in Public Life,* Robert A Katzmann (ed.), pp. 172-178. Baltimore, MD: Johns Hopkins University Press.

Index